YOU CAN PAINT

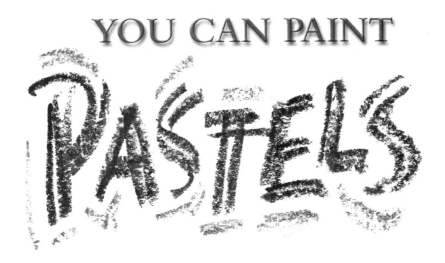

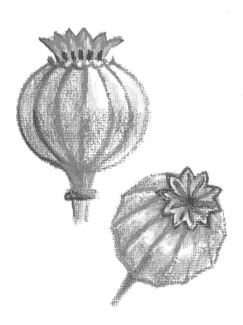

MARIE BLAKE trained as a painter at Kingston-upon-
Thames School of Art and later qualified as a teacher
of art at Central College, London University. She has
taught art at the primary and secondary levels and has
also led workshops. She exhibits her paintings and is
a regular contributor to *Leisure Painter* magazine.
This is her first book.

YOU CAN PAINT

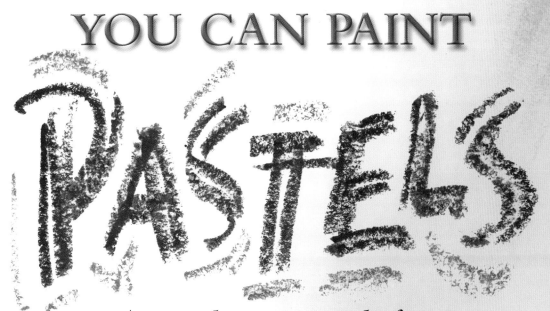

PASTELS

A step-by-step guide for
ABSOLUTE BEGINNERS

MARIE BLAKE

Watson-Guptill Publications/New York

First published in the United States in 2000 by
Watson-Guptill Publications, a division of
BPI Communications, Inc.
770 Broadway, New York, NY 10003
www.watsonguptill.com

Library of Congress Card Number: 00-104484

ISBN 0-8230-5990-1

First published in the United Kingdom in 2000 by
HarperCollins*Publishers*
77-85 Fulham Palace Road
Hammersmith
London W6 8JB

Editorial Director: Cathy Gosling
Editor: Diana Vowles
Designer: Penny Dawes
Photography: Nigel Cheffers-Heard

Color reproduction by Colourscan, Singapore
Printed and bound by Rotolito Lombarda SpA, Italy

1 2 3 4 5 6 7 / 06 05 04 03 02 01 00

CONTENTS

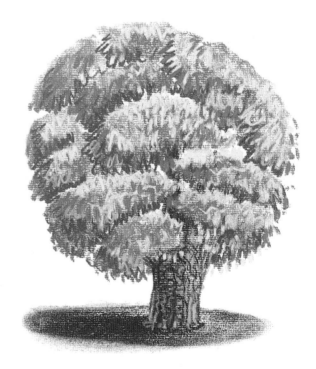

INTRODUCTION

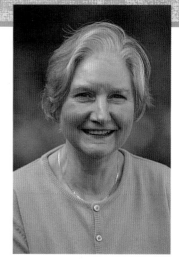

I t is not uncommon for people to feel that they would love to paint but lack sufficient knowledge and time. There is the question of what to choose from a bewildering range of brushes, pigments, and papers, as well as the numerous accessories that seem to be required.

There is no need for such apprehensions with pastels; they do not depend on tools and solvents, being simply paints in dry stick form, ready for immediate use. As soon as you open a box of pastels, your fingers will itch to handle the various colors and make tentative scribbles to see how they respond—and at that moment you will already have started to paint. Perhaps it is their resemblance to the boxes of crayons we are given in childhood, when our creative impulses are not inhibited by our fear of failure, that makes pastels seem so accessible to use.

The making of marks is a basic human compulsion, and if it is exercised regularly, your hands will learn to respond automatically, giving you the freedom to paint creatively. Right from your first experiments in pastel you will find yourself making lines that are as fine as pencil marks and broad masses similar to brush strokes. These discoveries allow you to develop your drawing and painting skills simultaneously, an advantage that pastels are unique in offering.

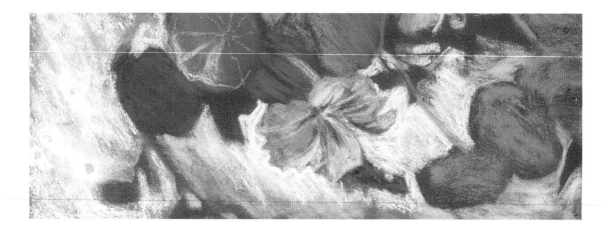

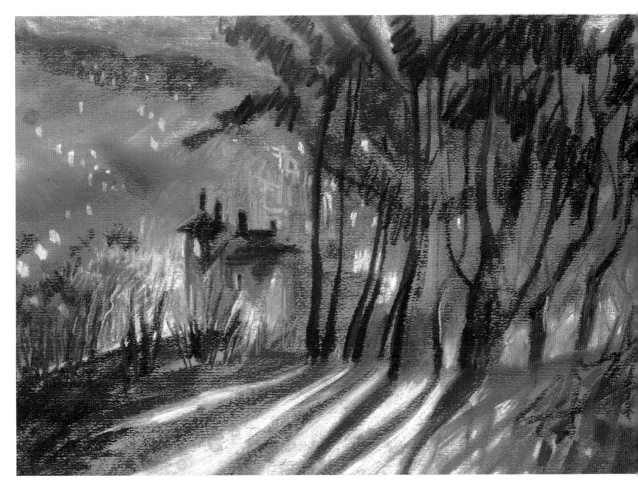

Through the Garden at Night
11½ x 8″

Being able to paint successfully depends upon being able to draw, and drawing in its turn depends upon being able to see objects in a different manner from the practical everyday method. This "reflex drawing" produces a natural way of working that is both relaxing and fun. It is also the basis of this book.

On the same principle of working freely, do not be concerned about other people's reactions to your early paintings. If you aim to please others, you will be depriving yourself of valuable learning experience. There is tactile as well as visual satisfaction to be had from painting with pastels, and even the most basic exercise will express the pleasure you feel when you paint in pastels just for yourself.

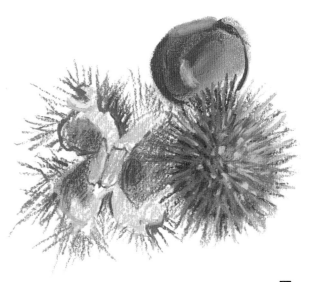

You can paint **7**

HOW TO USE THIS BOOK

This book is designed to teach you by presenting images for you to work with and then develop further yourself. The early pages are devoted to basic mark-making, which will teach you to how to handle pastels. Once you are familiar with their use, you can tackle the exercises in reflex drawing and painting; these will teach you how to allow the pastel in your fingers to follow the rhythm of the scene while you use your eyes to study what is before you, rather than anxiously watching what is appearing on the paper.

Of course, to paint successfully you must understand how to use color. On pages 22–29, you will learn about color relationships so that

Beach Huts out of Season
8¼ x 10¼"

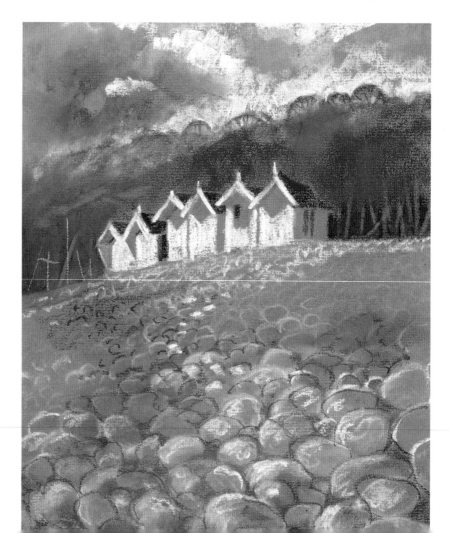

you will be able to make the right choices of which pastels to buy and how to mix them to achieve the effects you want.

Choosing interesting subjects and handling them to absorb their tactile quality is an important part of painting. Once you have progressed through the basic exercises, this book offers you the chance to practice the portrayal of subjects from nature such as trees, flowers, and the seashore, as well as the people and animals that give life to a landscape.

The book is intended to give you an enjoyable start in the use of pastel, a fulfilling and exciting medium. It does not cover subjects such as linear perspective, which require more practice. Instead, it shows you how to make pictures from straightforward viewpoints, so that right from the start you can produce work that will inspire you to explore pastels further, rather than feeling discouraged about your abilities. It opens a new world that offers fun as well as creative fulfillment—and further adventure to be had as your skills develop.

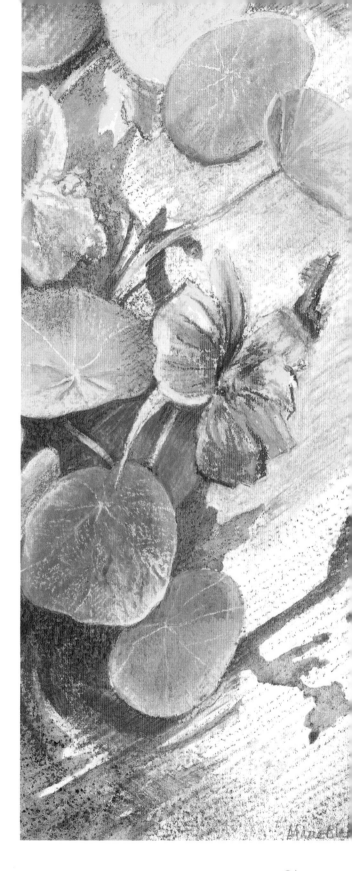

Nasturtiums and Shadows
5 x 11¾"

BASIC MATERIALS

As a beginner, it is easy to equip yourself for painting with pastels without a great deal of outlay or research. In fact, just six pastels and a sketchbook will suffice to allow you the chance to discover whether you wish to explore this exciting medium further.

The pastels   There is a vast range of pastels on the market. The color names I refer to in this book are those used by Daler-Rowney, but the brand you choose is not very important. Just match the colors shown in the exercises as closely as you can with the colors you have

purchased. Each pastel color comes in a range of values—usually from three to eight different shades. The approximate value of each color I use is indicated in parentheses after the color name.

Pastels also come in different shapes. Round pastels are soft and produce the most painterly effect, while square pastels are firmer and good for linear detail. Pastel pencils are the cleanest to hold.

To begin with, buy six basic colors: two reds, two blues, and two yellows. Choose a warm and a cool shade in each. You can either buy them loose or, if you are willing to spend more money, as part of a set. Once you have completed the section on color mixing (pages 22–29) you can make your own personal selection of the colors that will suit your style.

Preliminary studies and initial drawings can be done in charcoal, an inexpensive medium.

Pastel papers   These have a textured surface to hold the pastel particles. They are available in a large range of colors, whether as loose sheets or as pads of assorted colors. White papers can be used for studies, but mid-toned colored papers are easiest for painting. A useful size is 9 x 12″.

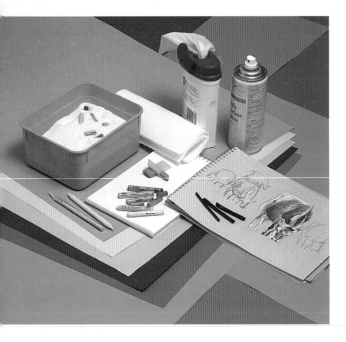

All the basic equipment you need to start painting in pastels.

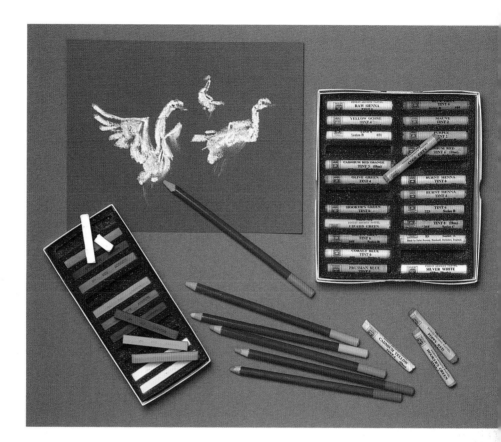

A selection of round and square pastels and pastel pencils.

A spiral-bound sketchbook of 6 x 9″ is suitable for outdoor work. Sketchbooks are supplied with white, cream, or colored paper. The pages are interleaved to prevent the pastel from smudging the adjoining page.

Optional extras If you do not wish to use your finger for blending, use paper towel. It can be rolled into "tortillons" to blend areas too small for a finger. You can also purchase tortillons at art supply stores. When the point of a tortillon needs to be cleaned, sharpen it with a craft knife. The latter is also useful for sharpening pastels.

Pastel paintings are fragile, but you can "fix" them by covering them with smooth paper and placing them under a heavy board. Alternatively, use aerosol fixative, following the manufacturer's instructions. Do not apply it heavily or it will darken the colors, and use it only in a well-ventilated room.

An eraser is used for lifting color to leave highlights, not for correcting mistakes. Buy either a kneaded eraser or one made of good-quality plastic—not a rubber one. To lift narrow lines, simply cut the eraser into thin strips.

To clean your fingers, use moist wipes or a damp sponge. Pastels can be cleaned by shaking them gently in a container of ground rice, available from health food stores.

MAKING MARKS

Before you can learn to paint successfully, you need to find pleasure in just making marks. Here are a few suggestions on which to base your inventiveness. You will need two pastels, fixative, a tortillon, an eraser, paper towel, and white pastel paper (see pages 8–11).

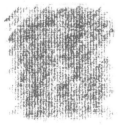

*Make a light stroke (**left**); break the pastel and use its sharp edge for a thin line (**center**); drag a wide band with its full length (**right**).*

Repeat using increased pressure.

Make three horizontal strokes, graduating from heavy to light.

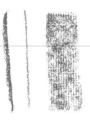

Apply diagonal stripes (known as "close-hatching" or "infill").

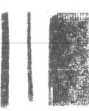

Repeat and blend by rubbing gently with paper towel.

Repeat and blend with a finger.

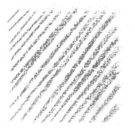

Make diagonal spaced blue lines ("hatching").

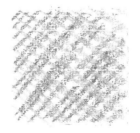

"Crosshatch" in the opposite direction with yellow.

Use a finger to blend the yellow into the blue.

Drag a band of blue next to a band of yellow. Blend them together with your finger.

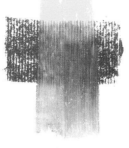

Drag a blue horizontal band, then cross it with a vertical yellow band. Notice the color blend.

Repeat, but spray with fixative before applying yellow. Notice the color separation.

Heavily infill in blue, then finger-blend gently to obscure the individual strokes.

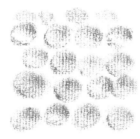

Transfer the color left on your finger to make a fingerprint texture.

Alternatively, rub the color into the paper to give a diffused texture.

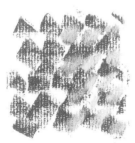

Make blunt stipple marks with a short length of blue pastel, then overlay them with yellow.

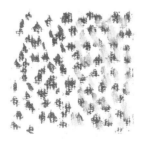

Make sharp stipple marks in blue, then in yellow.

Gently flick feathering strokes in blue, followed by yellow.

From marks to shapes

As you continue to experiment with making marks you will find that some of them spontaneously begin to take on recognizable shapes, in the same way that idle doodles invariably turn into faces and forms rather than remaining meaningless scribbles.

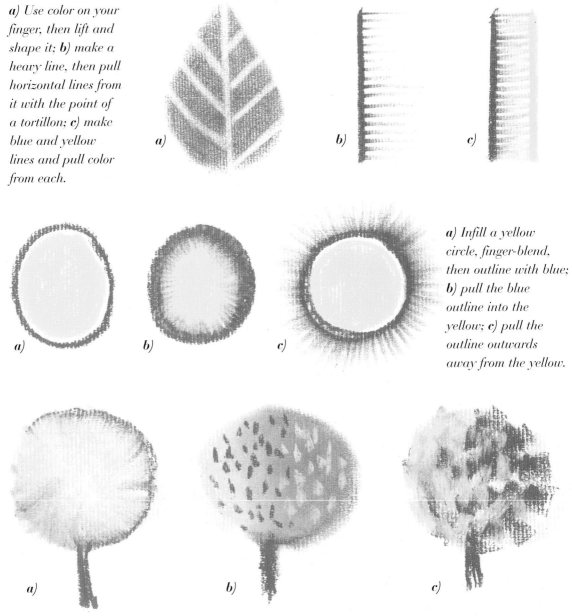

a) Use color on your finger, then lift and shape it; b) make a heavy line, then pull horizontal lines from it with the point of a tortillon; c) make blue and yellow lines and pull color from each.

a) Infill a yellow circle, finger-blend, then outline with blue; b) pull the blue outline into the yellow; c) pull the outline outwards away from the yellow.

Using the techniques you have learned so far, make your first basic pictures by a) pulling an outline and infilling with yellow; b) blending one color into another and stippling over the top; c) making blunt stipple marks with a short length of pastel.

Toned papers

Colored paper is the traditional surface for pastels. It saves you from having to cover the whole surface, and is therefore cleaner and more economical to use than white paper. More importantly, it helps you to achieve a balance of light and dark in a picture by establishing a middle tone.

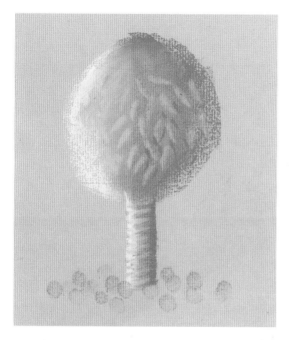

Left: Here the background is light in tone, yet dark enough for the light left-hand side of the tree to be more visible than it would have appeared on white paper.

Below: The same tree on a mid-toned paper that lowers the contrast between the background and the light and dark sides of the tree.

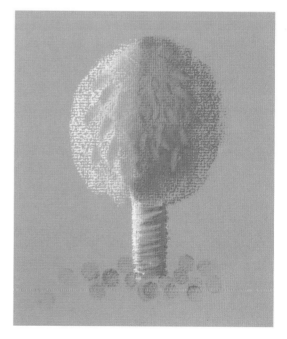

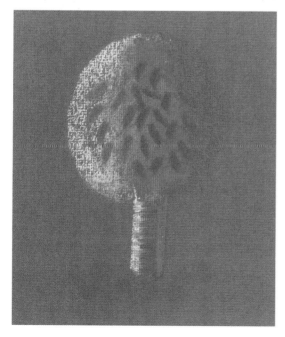

Left: Here the paper is too dark in tone, with the result that the right-hand side of the tree has merged into the background.

Drawing with your eyes shut

You cannot paint without drawing, and this is especially true when you're using pastels. These preliminary exercises are relaxing and fun, but are also significant in developing your drawing skills. Close your eyes for each exercise, then check the result before progressing to the next one.

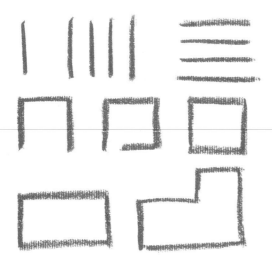

1 Top: a line; four equally spaced vertical parallel lines; four horizontal parallel lines. Center: three sides of a square; a square drawn in a continuous line, the last edge falling short; a perfect square. Bottom: a rectangle; a right-angled irregular shape.

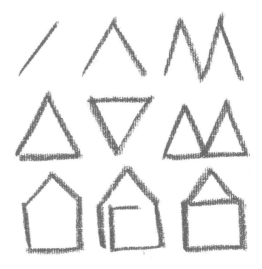

2 Top: a diagonal line; two sides of a triangle; the letter M. Center: a triangle; an inverted triangle; a double triangle. Bottom: an open triangle on an open square; two house shapes.

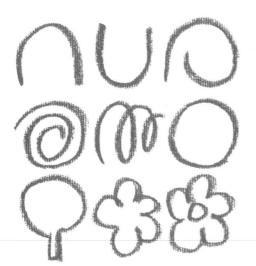

3 Top: a downward curve; an upward curve; a scroll. Center: a curl; a spring; a circle. Bottom: a tree shape; a flower shape; a flower with a center.

Painting with your eyes shut

When you have had plenty of practice with the drawing exercises on the previous page, you can move on to painting with a short length of pastel. As before, the exercises are based on squares, triangles and circles.

1 *Top: With the pastel held horizontally as shown, pull three strokes; pull one long vertical stroke; push, with a final move to the right.* **Center:** *With the pastel held vertically, make three left-to-right strokes; one long left-to-right stroke; and one left-to-right stroke with a final upward movement.* **Bottom:** *Mixed vertical and horizontal strokes.*

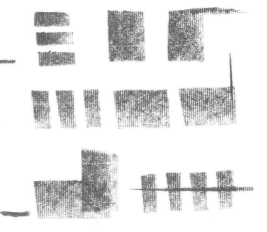

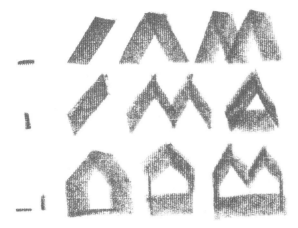

2 *Holding the pastel horizontally or vertically as indicated, follow the push, pull, right, or left movements in the illustrations.*

3 *Top: With the pastel held horizontally, push and pull in one smooth movement; pull and push; push, pull, and push.* **Center:** *With the pastel held vertically, push and pull; pull and push; push, pull, and finish with a push.* **Bottom:** *With the pastel held vertically, push, pull, and complete the circle; repeat horizontally; repeat with the pastel held at an oblique angle.*

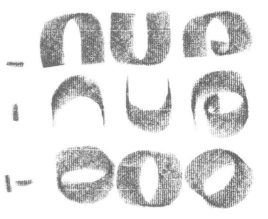

Basic images

The square and circular shapes from the previous exercises are used in this basic drawing, which is also to be done with your eyes closed. Practice it several times, then invent a design of your own, including some triangular shapes.

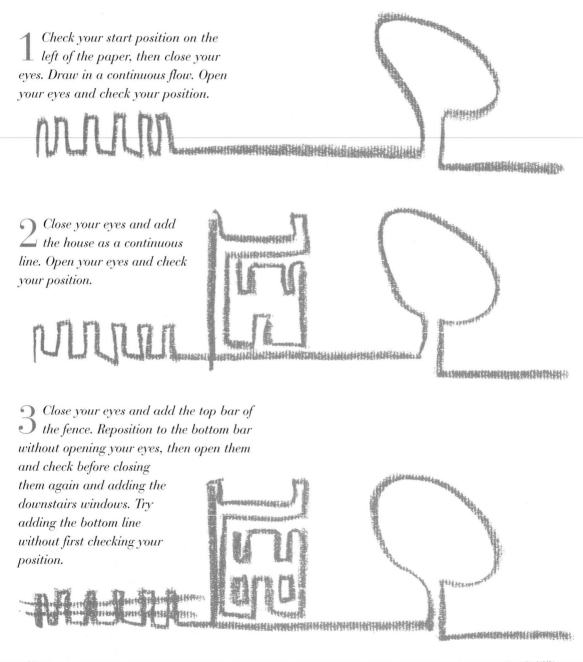

1 *Check your start position on the left of the paper, then close your eyes. Draw in a continuous flow. Open your eyes and check your position.*

2 *Close your eyes and add the house as a continuous line. Open your eyes and check your position.*

3 *Close your eyes and add the top bar of the fence. Reposition to the bottom bar without opening your eyes, then open them and check before closing them again and adding the downstairs windows. Try adding the bottom line without first checking your position.*

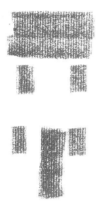

1 Using a short length of pastel, make two sideways sweeps for the roof and four short sideways marks for the windows. Turn the pastel and pull it towards you for a door. Practice before proceeding to the next step.

2 Make a tree with a curling movement followed by a straight pull. Relocate for a baseline beneath the picture. Practice, then fix the pastel before proceeding to step 3.

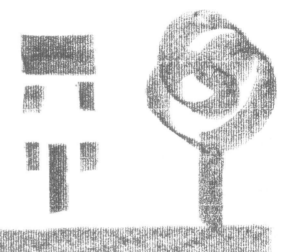

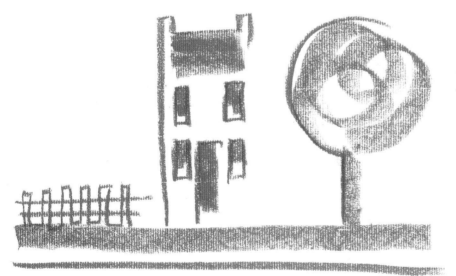

3 Change color and, using the pastel point, add the fence. Open your eyes, check, then close them and add the outlines of the house. Open your eyes, check, then close them and add an outline to the tree. Add the baseline without opening your eyes.

You can paint 19

Reflex drawing

Once you have discovered your ability to draw "blind," your eyes are free to observe objects without being distracted or inhibited by the marks you make on the paper. Reflex drawing teaches the automatic response of hand to eye that gives vitality to a painting.

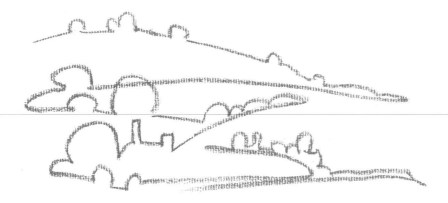

1 *Starting at the top left, follow a line to the right, then continue down to the next line and work right to left. Work continuously back and forth to the bottom (foreground).*

2 *Work as in the first step, beginning at the top left and drawing your line back and forth towards the bottom.*

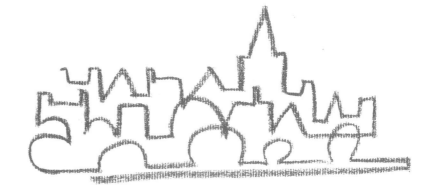

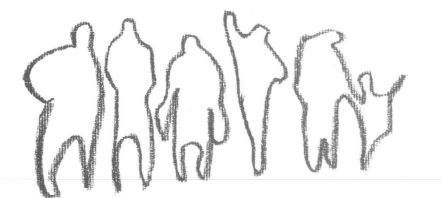

3 *When drawing moving people, your eye is more concerned with gesture than with detail. If you use a small sketchbook, no one will notice what you are doing.*

Reflex painting

Similar to reflex drawing but using a broader method, reflex painting is a useful way of making a quick statement of shapes and giving simple color reference. Begin by using one color, then progress to three as you gain confidence. Adapt my procedure to subject matter you can observe.

1 *With my eyes on the landscape, I applied yellow, then took a quick look at the paper. Looking back to the scene I applied green, checked its position, then incorporated the line and added the red detail.*

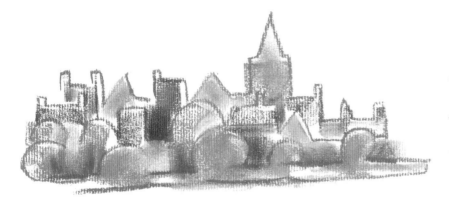

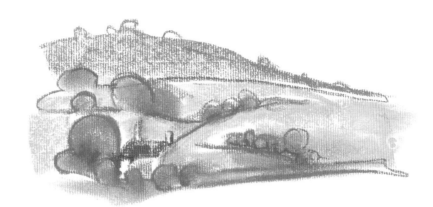

2 *Again, I applied yellow first, then green, and finally red, checking my position on the paper after using each color. I looked at the paper while I added the line.*

3 *As before, the colors were put in working from light to dark, checking positions before switching colors. Line was added only where the colors did not describe the shapes unaided.*

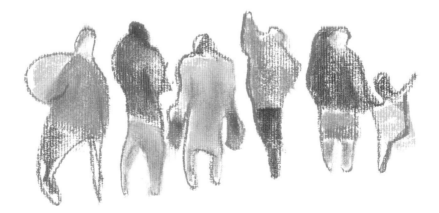

COLOR MIXING

Pastel is a dry medium with an extensive choice of ready-made colors. However, if you have never mixed colors and do not understand the relationships that exist between them, you will not be able to select or use ready-made colors successfully.

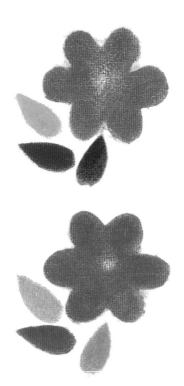

Orange is a secondary color made from warm yellow and warm red. Apply it thinly for a pale color. Add a touch of blue and use it thinly for a grayed orange or densely for a brown.

Red, cool or warm, is a primary color. Apply it thinly for pink. If you add a touch of green (a mixture of blue and yellow) and use it thinly, you'll get a grayed pink. Apply the same mixture densely for dark red.

Purple is a secondary color made from cool red and warm blue. Apply it thinly for a lilac and densely for a darker shade.

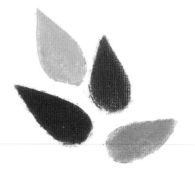

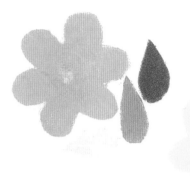

Yellow, cool or warm, is a primary color. Apply it thinly for a pale yellow. Add a touch of purple (red and blue) and use it thinly for a grayed yellow or densely for darkened yellow.

Green is a secondary color made from cool blue and cool yellow. Apply it thinly for a pale green. Add a touch of red and use it thinly for grayed green or densely for dark green.

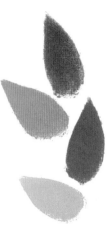

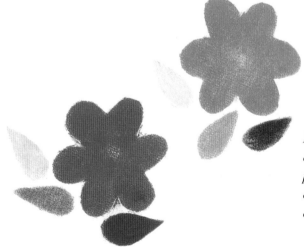

Blue is a primary color. Buy a warm and a cool blue. Apply color thinly for pale blue. Add small amounts of red and yellow for dark blue. Apply darkened blue thinly for gray.

Color exercises

With these exercises you will create your own colors from two blues, two yellows, and two reds. They will show you how colors relate and provide guidance when you shop for pastels. I made flower shapes, but you may wish to work more simply. The color names are for guidance only.

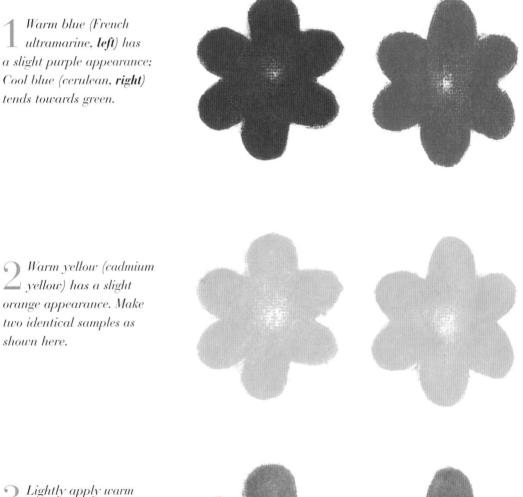

1 *Warm blue (French ultramarine, **left**) has a slight purple appearance; Cool blue (cerulean, **right**) tends towards green.*

2 *Warm yellow (cadmium yellow) has a slight orange appearance. Make two identical samples as shown here.*

3 *Lightly apply warm blue, overlay with warm yellow, and blend (**left**). Lightly apply cool blue, overlay with warm yellow, and blend (**right**).*

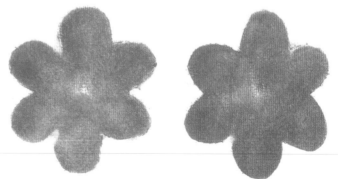

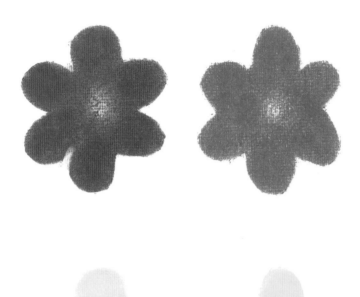

1 *Warm and cool blue, as shown in step 1 on the facing page.*

2 *Cool yellow (lemon yellow) has a tendency towards green. Make two identical samples as shown here.*

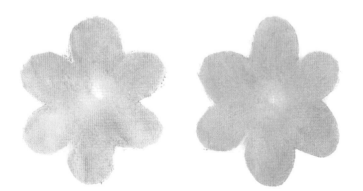

3 *Lightly apply warm blue, overlay with cool yellow, and blend (**left**). Lightly apply cool blue, overlay with cool yellow, and blend (**right**). The purest greens are made from cool blues mixed with cool yellows.*

On the previous two pages you learned how a permutation of blues and yellows will create a choice of greens. Use the same procedure with reds and yellows to make oranges. Lay a lighter color over a darker one, as it will make them easier to blend, and apply darker colors less generously.

1 *Cool red (rose madder) has a purple bias. Make two identical samples as shown.*

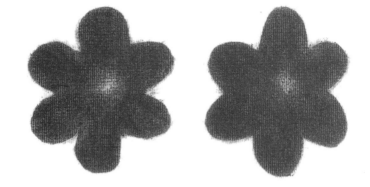

2 *Make samples of warm yellow (cadmium yellow, **left**) and cool yellow (lemon yellow, **right**).*

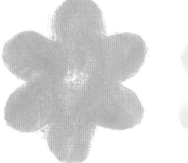

3 *Lightly apply cool red, overlay with warm yellow, and blend (**left**). Lightly apply cool red, overlay with cool yellow, and blend (**right**).*

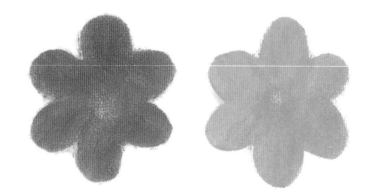

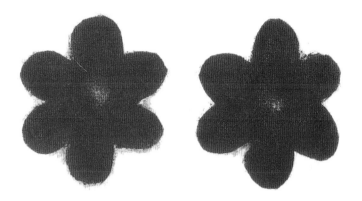

1 *Warm red (poppy red) has an orange bias. Make two identical samples as shown here.*

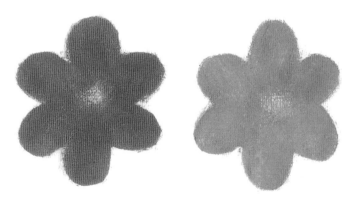

2 *Make samples of warm yellow and cool yellow as on the facing page.*

3 *Lightly apply warm red, overlay with warm yellow, and blend (**left**). Lightly apply warm red, overlay with cool yellow, and blend. You have now made four varieties of orange.*

These color exercises require time and effort, but once they are completed you will not need to mix your own pastel colors again: you will be able to buy them ready-made. armed with the knowledge of how to select them and how to compose a color scheme.

1 *Make two identical samples of cool blue (cerulean)as shown here.*

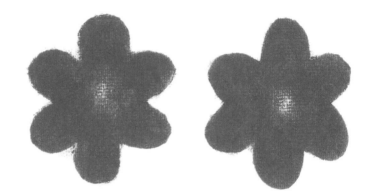

2 *Make samples of warm red (poppy red, **left**) and cool red (rose madder, **right**).*

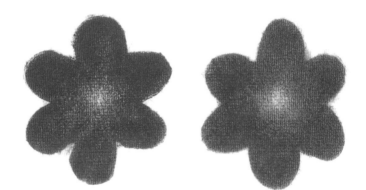

3 *Lightly apply cool blue, overlay with warm red, and blend (**left**). Lightly apply cool blue, overlay with cool red, and blend (**right**). Green-blue and orange-red contain traces of yellow, so they make a purple-brown.*

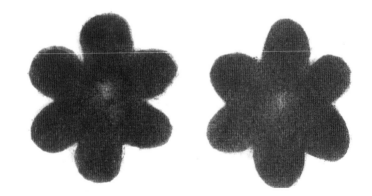

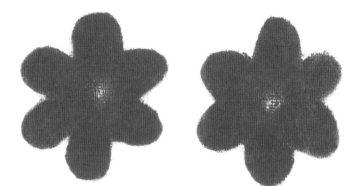

1 *Make two identical samples of warm blue (French ultramarine) as shown here.*

2 *Make samples of warm red and cool red as on the facing page.*

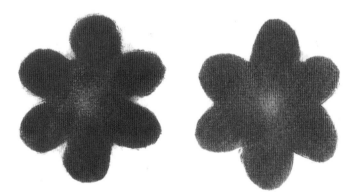

3 *Lightly apply warm blue, overlay with warm red, and blend (**left**). Lightly apply warm blue, overlay with cool red, and blend (**right**). A cool red and a warm blue make the clearest purple.*

FOREGROUND & DISTANCE

A piece of paper is two-dimensional—it has only height and width. The challenge of painting is to create the illusion of depth, giving it the three-dimensional appearance of reality. You can do this by employing both differences in scale and advancing (warm) and receding (cool) colors.

Identical objects

To practice creating an impression of depth in your picture, it is best to begin by experimenting with objects that are of identical size and a simple shape.

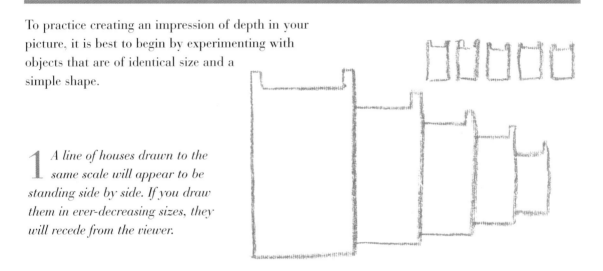

1 A line of houses drawn to the same scale will appear to be standing side by side. If you draw them in ever-decreasing sizes, they will recede from the viewer.

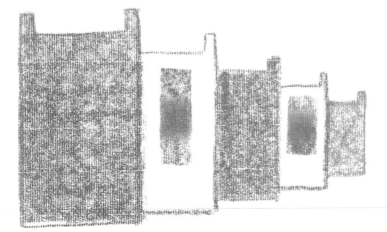

2 Accentuate the effect by using warm colors in the foreground, progressing to cool colors in the background. From the foreground, the sequence here is burnt sienna, blended ochre, sap green, blended viridian, and cerulean.

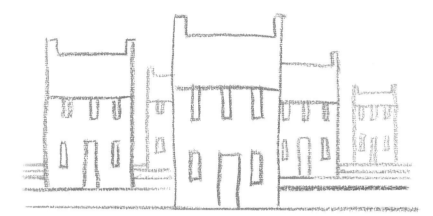

3 *Here the houses are arranged more informally. Each one stands on a baseline, and as they recede the space between the baselines diminishes.*

4 *The blue line represents your eyeline, which in this instance goes through the upper windows of each house. It shows that the houses are of similar size and are on level ground. Such construction lines can be erased when they are no longer needed.*

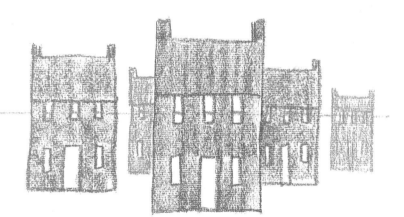

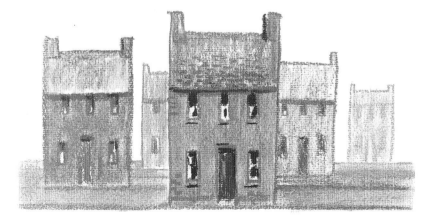

5 *Detail and contrast become more indistinct with distance. It helps here to view the subject with your eyes half-closed.*

LIGHT, SHADE, & SHAPE

The depiction of light and shade (tone) helps the viewer's eye to recognize objects and adds solidity to their forms. However, painting is made easier if at first you ignore the question of tone and concentrate upon finding the basic shapes of the objects.

From squares to cylinders

Shapes distort when viewed from above or below, so it is advisable for beginners to choose a central eyeline, indicated here by a blue line.

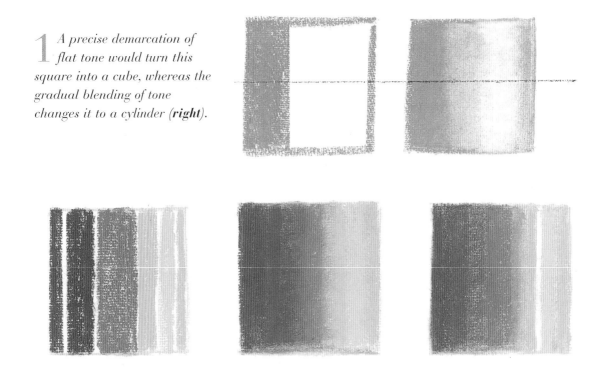

*1 A precise demarcation of flat tone would turn this square into a cube, whereas the gradual blending of tone changes it to a cylinder (**right**).*

*2 For a cylindrical shape, paint a wide band of color. Add progressively darker or lighter narrowing bands on each side (**left**)* *and blend. Solid color gives the appearance of a matte surface (**center**), while leaving some white paper gives a glossy effect (**right**).*

Triangles, pyramids, and cones

Like squares, cubes, and cylinders, triangular shapes distort when seen from an angle. Again, choose a central view as shown here by the blue line.

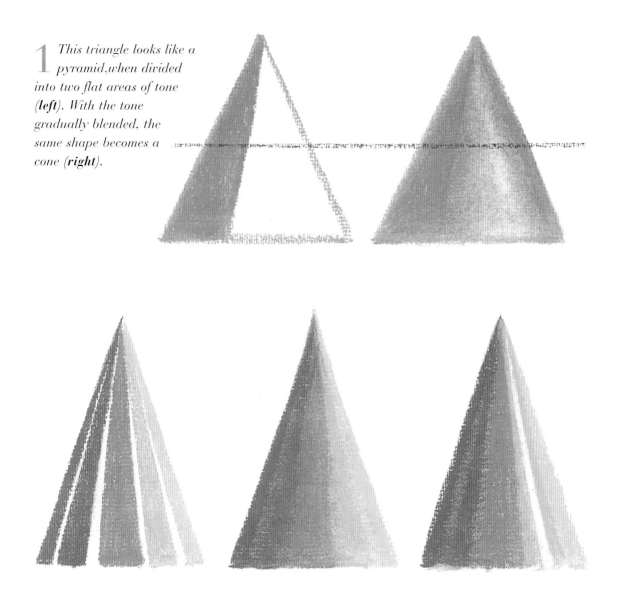

1 *This triangle looks like a pyramid,when divided into two flat areas of tone* (**left**). *With the tone gradually blended, the same shape becomes a cone* (**right**).

2 *Tonal changes radiate from the top of a cone. Place the widest central band of color first, followed by the lightest and darkest tones on either side* (**left**). *Blend the colors, covering the paper entirely for a matte surface* (**center**) *and allowing some white paper to show through to give the appearance of a glossy surface* (**right**).

Circles and spheres

Unlike square and triangular shapes, circular objects retain their shape whatever position they are viewed from. Consequently, there is no need to establish a particular eye level.

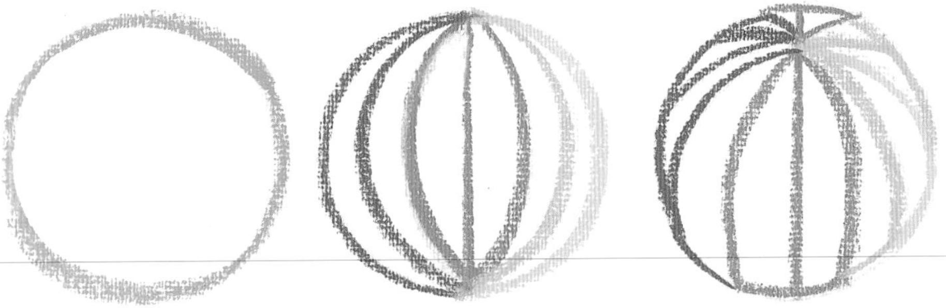

*1 Draw a circle, then add sections on either side of a central axis (**center**) or radiate them from any point, flattening them on the opposite side (**far right**).*

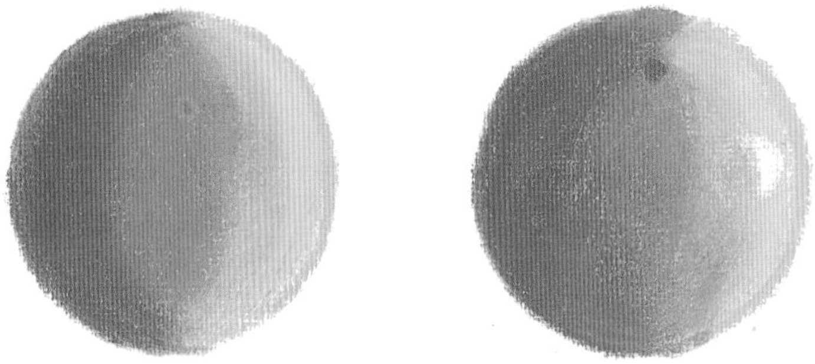

*2 Infill the colors, graduating the tone and covering the paper entirely for a matte surface (**left**) or lifting a highlight for a glossy one (**right**).*

3 The angle of light from the top of an object to its baseline will determine the length of a cast shadow. The illustration on the left shows the shadow cast at noon. In the illustration on the right, the time could be either mid-morning or mid-afternoon.

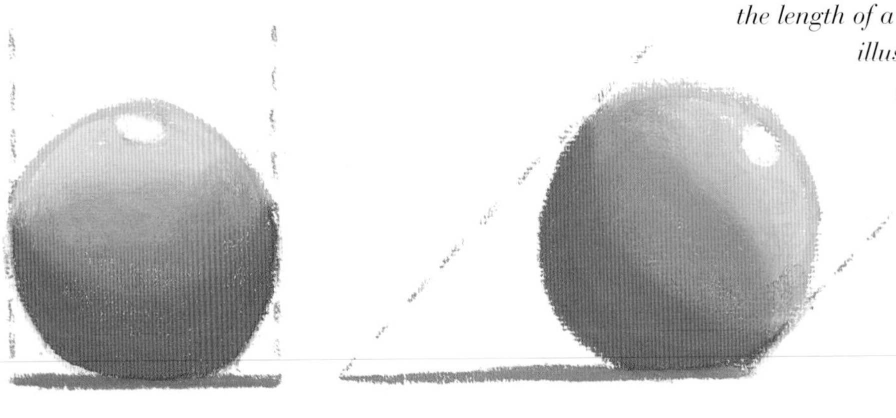

Combining shapes

Most objects are composed of a combination of triangular, rounded, and square shapes. Make diagrammatic drawings of the domestic items that surround you, taking care when establishing your eye level (shown here by a blue line).

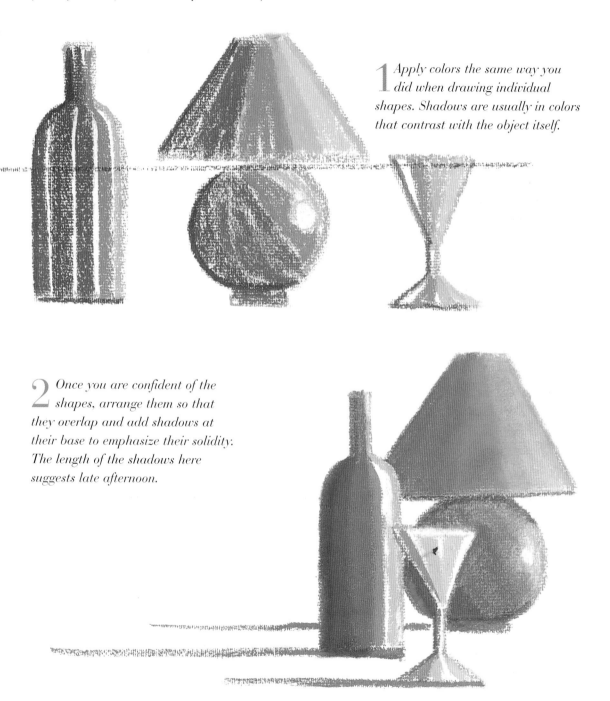

1 Apply colors the same way you did when drawing individual shapes. Shadows are usually in colors that contrast with the object itself.

2 Once you are confident of the shapes, arrange them so that they overlap and add shadows at their base to emphasize their solidity. The length of the shadows here suggests late afternoon.

EXPLORING PLANTS

Although a daisy may look very different from a rose, for example, leaves, petals, and stems share basic biological characteristics and structures. Begin by choosing simple shapes and making preliminary line drawings from a flat viewpoint. From there you can progress to more complex shapes and angles.

Simple leaves

Choose three tones of one color for this basic leaf shape. I have used yellow-green, but red or orange would be equally appropriate.

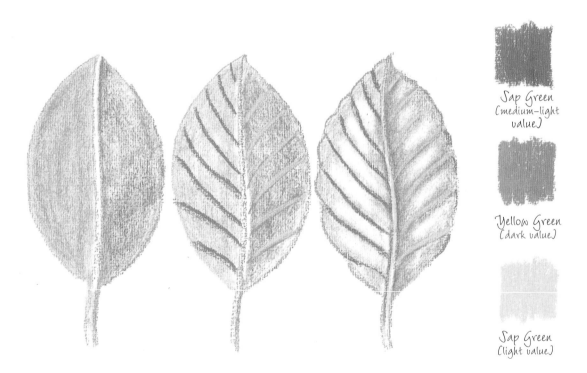

Sap Green
(medium-light
value)

Yellow Green
(dark value)

Sap Green
(light value)

*The crease along the central spine of a leaf creates a division between light and shade. Draw the shape first, fill with close hatching, and then fix (**left**). Next, draw the veins on* *either side, using dark on light and light on dark (**center**). If the surface of the leaf is glossy, lift out highlights between the veins using an eraser (**right**).*

Curving leaves

When leaves fold and curve. they show both their upper and under surfaces. If you observe them carefully. curving leaves are no more challenging to paint than flat leaves.

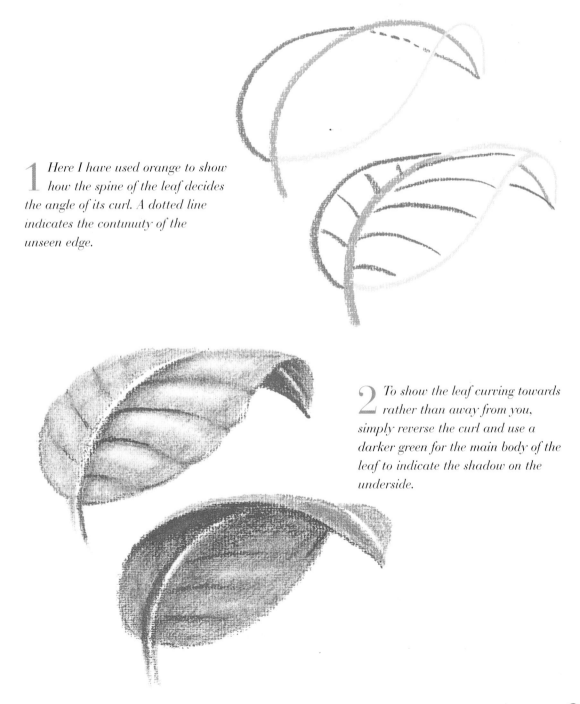

1 *Here I have used orange to show how the spine of the leaf decides the angle of its curl. A dotted line indicates the continuity of the unseen edge.*

2 *To show the leaf curving towards rather than away from you, simply reverse the curl and use a darker green for the main body of the leaf to indicate the shadow on the underside.*

Buds

Flower buds are enclosed by a case of leaves that protects the petals and seedpod. The volume of the closed bud also governs the shape of the subsequent seedpod.

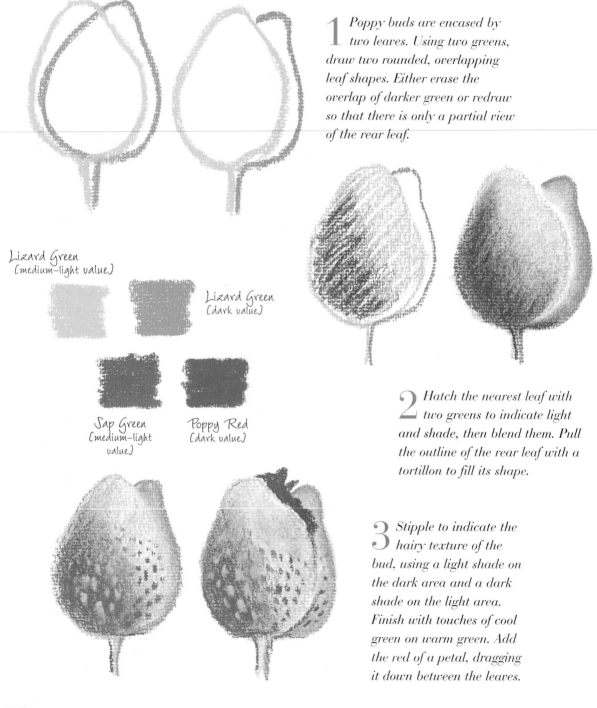

1 *Poppy buds are encased by two leaves. Using two greens, draw two rounded, overlapping leaf shapes. Either erase the overlap of darker green or redraw so that there is only a partial view of the rear leaf.*

Lizard Green
(medium-light value)

Lizard Green
(dark value)

Sap Green
(medium-light value)

Poppy Red
(dark value)

2 *Hatch the nearest leaf with two greens to indicate light and shade, then blend them. Pull the outline of the rear leaf with a tortillon to fill its shape.*

3 *Stipple to indicate the hairy texture of the bud, using a light shade on the dark area and a dark shade on the light area. Finish with touches of cool green on warm green. Add the red of a petal, dragging it down between the leaves.*

Seedpods

Many plants have seedpods that are very attractive and long-lasting when dried. However, you should compare a dried pod with its living equivalent in the center of a flower.

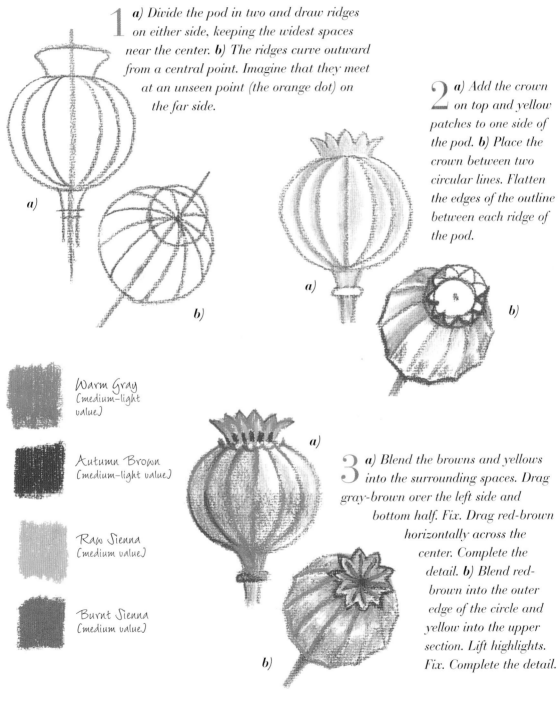

1 *a) Divide the pod in two and draw ridges on either side, keeping the widest spaces near the center. b) The ridges curve outward from a central point. Imagine that they meet at an unseen point (the orange dot) on the far side.*

2 *a) Add the crown on top and yellow patches to one side of the pod. b) Place the crown between two circular lines. Flatten the edges of the outline between each ridge of the pod.*

Warm Gray
(medium-light value)

Autumn Brown
(medium-light value)

Raw Sienna
(medium value)

Burnt Sienna
(medium value)

3 *a) Blend the browns and yellows into the surrounding spaces. Drag gray-brown over the left side and bottom half. Fix. Drag red-brown horizontally across the center. Complete the detail. b) Blend red-brown into the outer edge of the circle and yellow into the upper section. Lift highlights. Fix. Complete the detail.*

Petals

Petals take many forms, from the frilled, complex forms of the carnation to the simple saucer shapes of buttercups. However, they are rarely completely flat, so pay attention to how the light falls on them and alters their color.

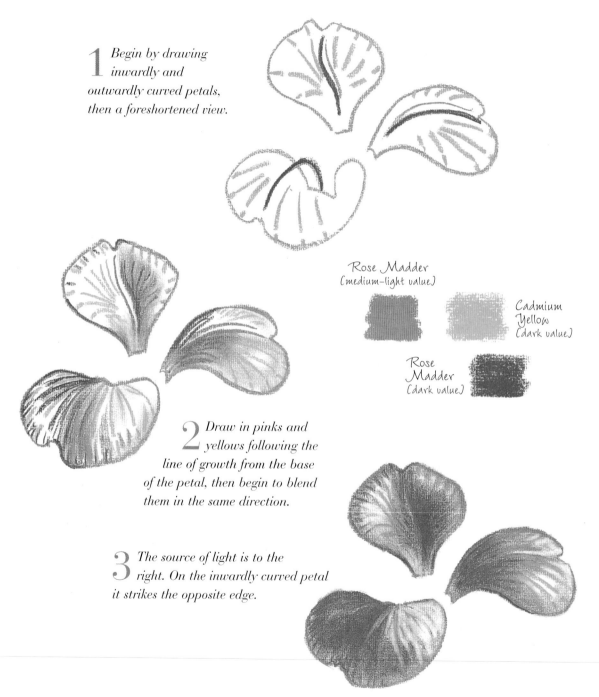

1 *Begin by drawing inwardly and outwardly curved petals, then a foreshortened view.*

Rose Madder
(medium-light value)

Cadmium
Yellow
(dark value)

Rose
Madder
(dark value)

2 *Draw in pinks and yellows following the line of growth from the base of the petal, then begin to blend them in the same direction.*

3 *The source of light is to the right. On the inwardly curved petal it strikes the opposite edge.*

Stems

A stem can be drawn in a line progressing from thick to thin in one quick movement. With your paper upside down, apply the pastel firmly, releasing pressure as you draw it towards you.

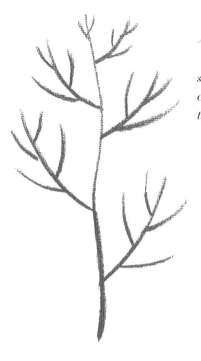

1 *Still working upside down, add alternating side stems. Make them closer together towards the top.*

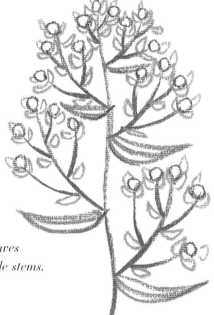

2 *Add leaves here and there where side stems branch from the main stem. Then, add more leaves at the junctions of the side stems.*

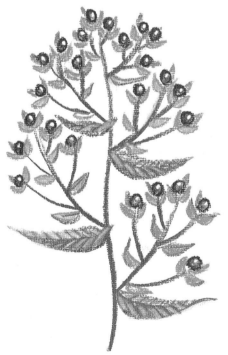

 Madder Brown (medium value)

 Madder Brown (medium-dark value)

 Cadmium Orange (dark value)

Raw Sienna (dark value)

3 *Buds, berries, seedpods, and flowers can be drawn at the tips of the stems, surrounded by clusters of small leaves.*

Aster

A many-petalled flower such as the aster is a little trickier than the trio of broad petals on page 40, but there is no need to include every detail. Once you have mastered the individual flower and are familiar with its form, trying painting the whole plant.

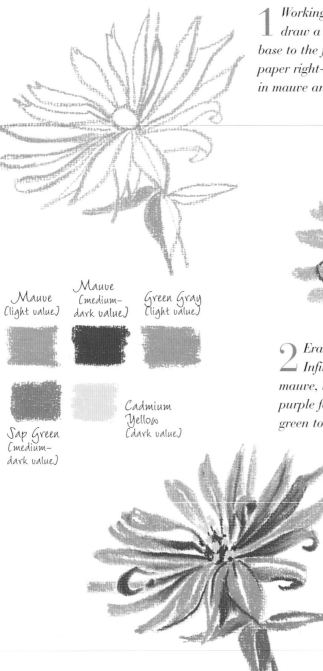

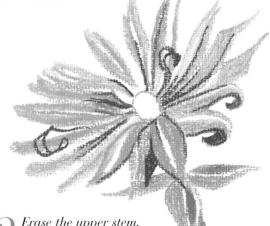

1 *Working upside down, lightly draw a gray-green stem from the base to the flower center. Turn your paper right-side up. Outline the petals in mauve and add the leaves.*

Mauve
(light value)

Mauve
(medium-dark value)

Green Gray
(light value)

Sap Green
(medium-dark value)

Cadmium Yellow
(dark value)

2 *Erase the upper stem. Infill the petals with mauve, leaving highlights. Use purple for shadows and add sap green to the leaves.*

3 *Make yellow dots for stamens and surround them with purple. Blend mauve into purple on the petals, but keep crisp edges on those facing forward.*

1 *Draw the branching stem in gray-green. Plot the positions of the flower heads so that they are seen full face, in profile, and from the rear. The outlines can be removed later with an eraser.*

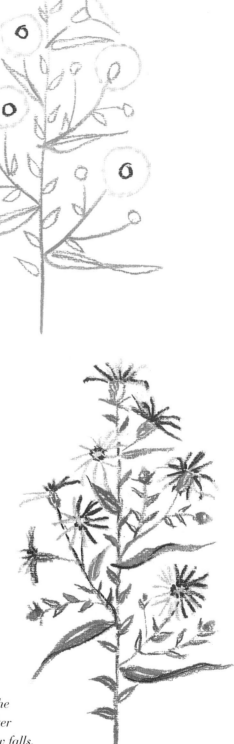

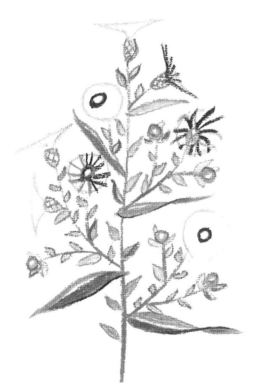

2 *Infill the small leaves on the side stems, as well as the larger ones at the junction of the stems. Crisscross the seedpods and begin to add structure to the flower heads.*

3 *Flesh out the detail on the flower heads, using darker mauve to show where shadow falls.*

Poppies

Poppies are endearingly attractive with their hairy stems, ragged leaves, and blowsy, crumpled petals, but beneath the apparent untidiness and fragility of the flowers there is a governing structure that you need to observe carefully.

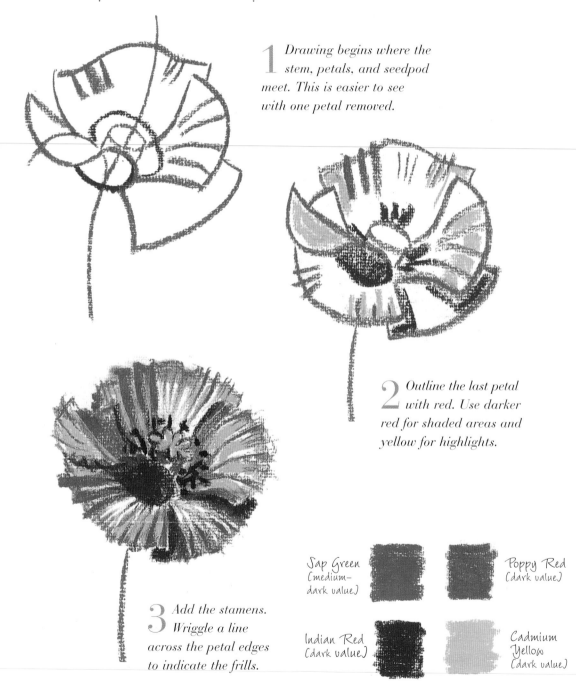

1 *Drawing begins where the stem, petals, and seedpod meet. This is easier to see with one petal removed.*

2 *Outline the last petal with red. Use darker red for shaded areas and yellow for highlights.*

3 *Add the stamens. Wriggle a line across the petal edges to indicate the frills.*

Sap Green
(medium-
dark value)

Poppy Red
(dark value)

Indian Red
(dark value)

Cadmium
Yellow
(dark value)

1 *You will find it easier to paint spiky poppy leaves if you first look at their underlying structure and placement on the stem. Near the top of the stem, the leaves are smaller.*

2 *With tracing paper, follow the lines of your initial drawing, adding spiky edges. Draw the tops of smaller leaves across the stem to indicate twists and turns.*

3 *Infill the greens, using a darker tone on the underside of the leaves where they are in shadow.*

4 *Now combine the flower with the leaves, remembering to start the flower with a single line of stem. Overlay it with the leaf stem, balanced in the opposite direction. Develop the leaf by adding a third green, but keep an open texture to suggest hairs. You can add these to the stem by lightly scratching with a knife.*

DEMONSTRATION ■ POPPY

AT A GLANCE...

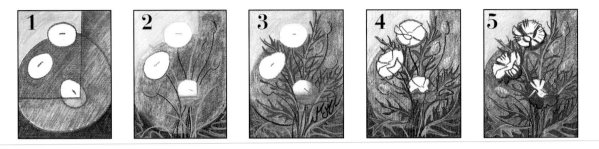

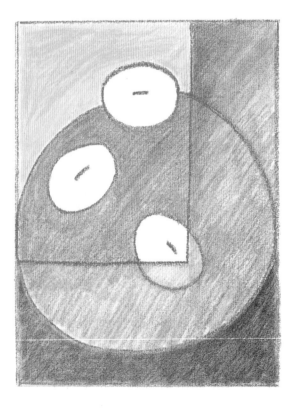

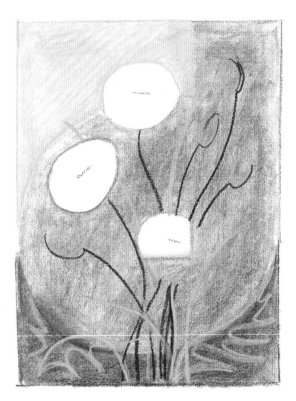

1 The main interest is created by contrasts, so extremes of red, green, light, and dark are concentrated in one area. The L shape created by the flowers is less significant. Drag and blend yellow, sap green, and olive green for the background.

2 Use olive green to draw the stems of buds and flowers and the edges of the buds that are farthest from the light. Draw the leaf stems and the outlines of buds in warm yellow. Use yellow-green for the leaves at the bottom.

The palette

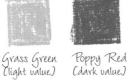

 Grass Green (light value)

 Poppy Red (dark value)

Indian Red (dark value)

Brilliant Green (dark value)

 Purple (medium value)

Cadmium Yellow (dark value)

 Olive Green (dark value)

 Sap Green (medium-light value)

 Lizard Green (medium-light value)

 Lemon Yellow (medium-light value)

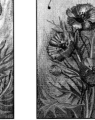

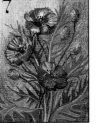

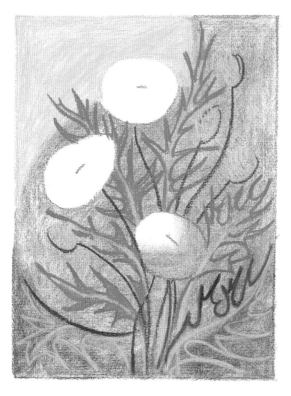

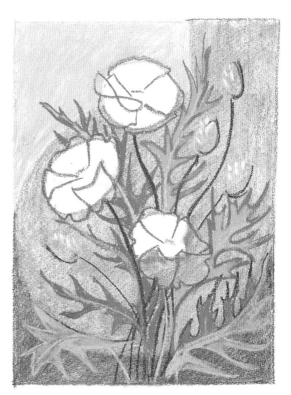

3 Draw the upper edges of the two foreground poppy leaves with olive green. Use sap green for the remaining leaves and infill the three on the left of the stem. Hatch the half of each bud that is nearest the light in yellow. Fix.

4 Highlight buds with lightest yellow. Partially infill foreground leaves with yellow-green. Complete the upper half of the leaf at bottom right with sap green, and the remaining leaves with a pale blue-green. Draw outlines of petals.

You can paint 47

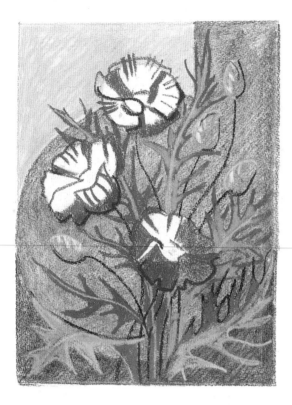

5 Infill a small area of sap green to the base of the left-hand foreground leaf. Infill the red of the poppies, leaving areas of white, and draw folds on the petals. Drag the pastel, allowing any green to show through, especially on the lowest flower. Outline shadow areas with dark red.

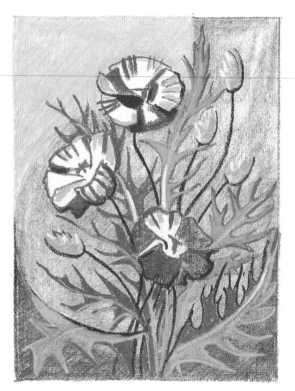

6 Blend and infill the dark red shadows. Place light blue-green on the shaded sides of the buds and use brightest green for the seedpods in each flower. Place reflected yellows between the folds of the petals and highlight the two leaf stems in the center of the picture with lightest yellow. Add red to the left-hand bud.

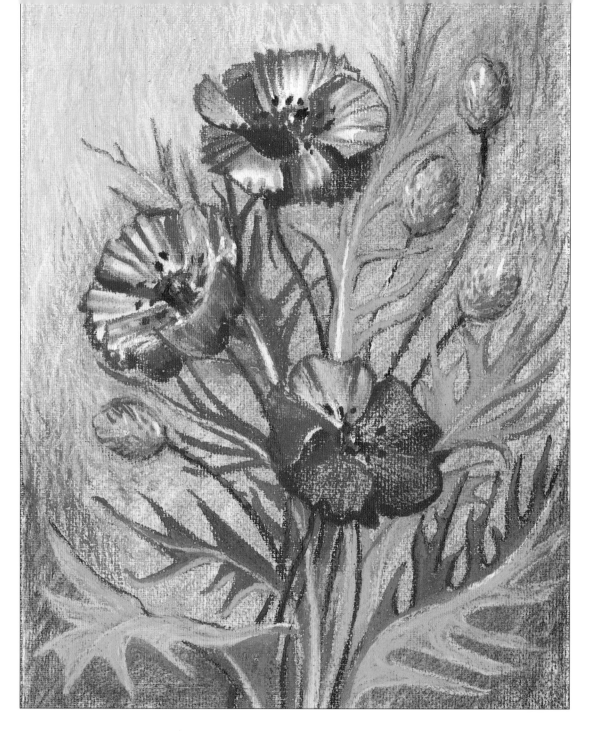

7 **_Finished picture_**: *8½ x 11½"*

Soften the background by feathering green on yellow and yellow on green so that edges blend. Stipple the buds and stems to give them texture and tone. Blend the leaves and the flowers. Stipple in the stamens and accentuate the contrasts of light and dark at the center of each flower, setting purple against white and brightest green against red.

Still life

The fruits and vegetables on these pages have been selected for their pattern or texture. Search out your own collection, choosing a variety of rough, smooth, ridged, or dimpled surfaces. Gourds, nuts, pinecones, and vegetables are all fruits of plants, so do not limit yourself to the grocery trade's definition of fruit.

Zucchini

No two zucchinis have the same pattern, and the one here looks as if it has scribbles on it as well as stripes. Notice how the pattern helps to describe the shape.

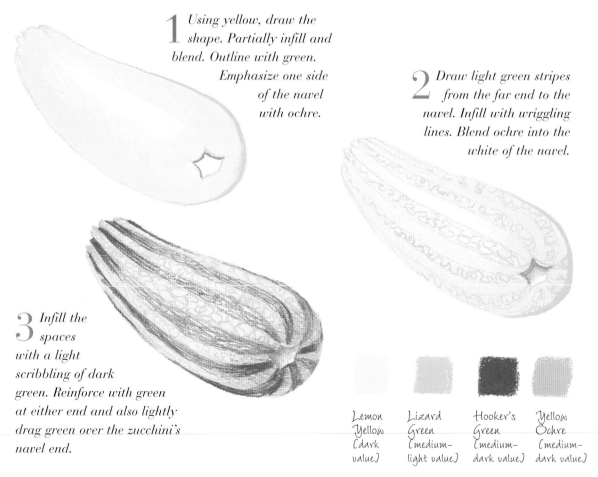

1 Using yellow, draw the shape. Partially infill and blend. Outline with green. Emphasize one side of the navel with ochre.

2 Draw light green stripes from the far end to the navel. Infill with wriggling lines. Blend ochre into the white of the navel.

3 Infill the spaces with a light scribbling of dark green. Reinforce with green at either end and also lightly drag green over the zucchini's navel end.

Lemon Yellow (dark value)

Lizard Green (medium-light value)

Hooker's Green (medium-dark value)

Yellow Ochre (medium-dark value)

Orange

Oranges are simple in shape; painting one is very much like doing the sphere exercise on page 34. However, you need to be careful when trying to create the textured feel of the skin, as casual stippling could have a flattening effect. Notice how the stippling is flatter and thinner at the circumference.

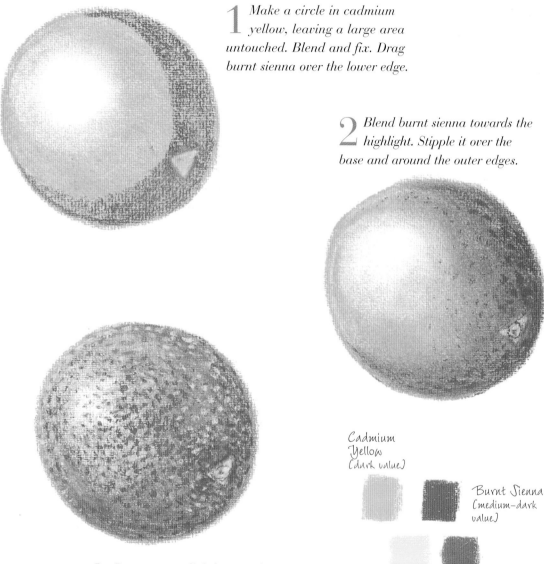

1 Make a circle in cadmium yellow, leaving a large area untouched. Blend and fix. Drag burnt sienna over the lower edge.

2 Blend burnt sienna towards the highlight. Stipple it over the base and around the outer edges.

3 Drag orange lightly over the upper half, then stipple it over the whole surface. Fix. Finally, stipple with lemon yellow.

Cadmium Yellow (dark value)

Burnt Sienna (medium-dark value)

Lemon Yellow (dark value)

Cadmium Tangerine (dark value)

Plums

Plums have no pattern to describe their shape and no obvious texture, but if you look carefully, you will often find that the skin has a bloom to it. This is texture in its subtlest form, shown by gently dragging a light color over a dark one.

1 *Drag a short length of red pastel in two overlapping ovals, then overlay with a partial outline in purple. From some viewpoints a plum displays distinct halves.*

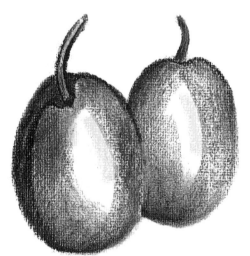

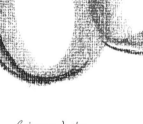

Crimson Lake
(medium–dark value)

Mauve
(medium–dark value)

Lemon Yellow
(dark value)

French Ultramarine
(light value)

2 *Add yellow in the highlights. Extend and deepen the red. Blend purple into the red, but maintain the crease. Draw yellow over the purple stalks in order to create a mix.*

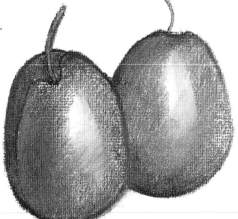

3 *Blend the red edges into the yellow and white, leaving a softer highlight. Fix. Drag a pale blue over all but the yellow-and-white area.*

Pinecone

Each of the examples of fruit has had either pattern or texture, but pinecones have both. Here the pattern not only describes the shape of the object, but also controls the way it feels. Handle pinecones before you begin to draw them so that you understand their texture.

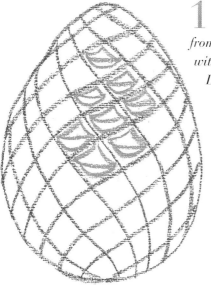

1 Draw a blue outline. Make curved stripes from top left, then cross with stripes from the right. Draw in arrow shapes.

2 Infill the spaces between the "arrows" with blue, covering the original lines. Drag and blend blue over the left side and base before infilling the "arrows" themselves.

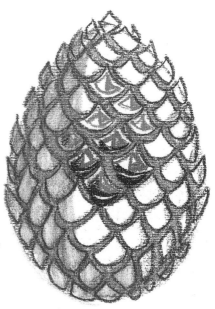

Prussian Blue
(medium-light value)

Cadmium Orange
(dark value)

Madder Brown
(dark value)

Cadmium Yellow
(dark value)

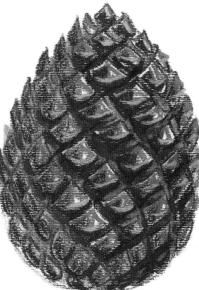

3 Fix, then apply outlines of orange, infilling to one side and underlining with brown. Emphasize the depths at the center of the cone with blue and highlight projections with yellow.

AT A GLANCE...

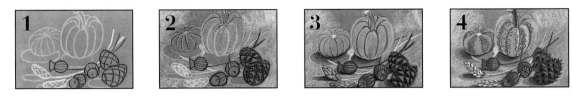

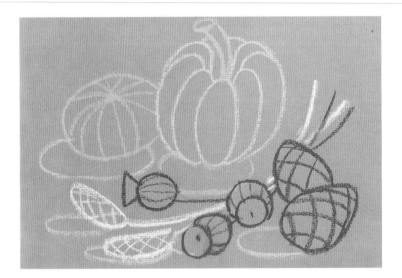

1 In a still life, you should arrange the objects so that interest is spread throughout the group. Here, the twisted stalk of the pumpkin directs the viewer's eye to the green gourd, from which the circular arrangement draws the eye through the wheat, poppy pods, and pinecones back to the starting point.

2 In this group, a green-yellow-orange harmony has been chosen, with dark purple as a contrast. Lightly infill the colors, leaving large areas of sand-colored paper showing. The color interest lies mainly in the large items in the upper section, while the darker tones at the bottom provide stability and weight.

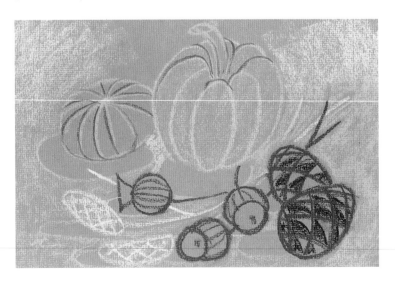

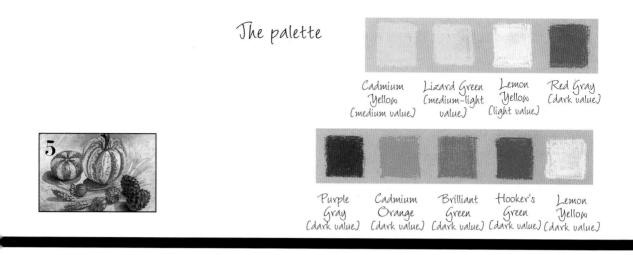

The palette

| Cadmium Yellow (medium value) | Lizard Green (medium-light value) | Lemon Yellow (light value) | Red Gray (dark value) |

| Purple Gray (dark value) | Cadmium Orange (dark value) | Brilliant Green (dark value) | Hooker's Green (dark value) | Lemon Yellow (dark value) |

3 Draw a purple-gray line under each object and blend it into the shadow area represented by blank paper. Blend the left half of each poppy pod to give them volume. Add linear detail to the pods and the wheat and intensify the colors of the pumpkin and gourd.

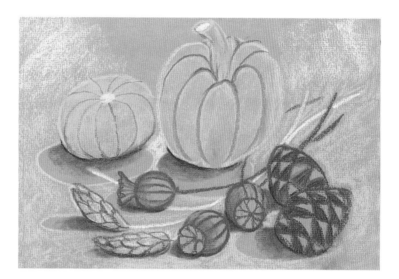

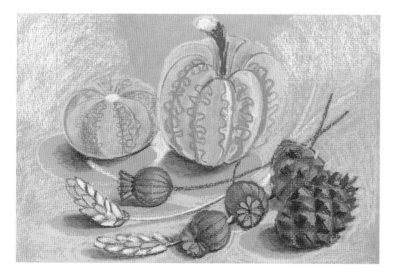

4 Blend the shadow area of each pinecone, intensify tonal contrasts, and create spikes by dragging the background color of the cones across the outer edges. Apply surface pattern to the pumpkin and gourd following the curving lines. Add purple detail to the seedpods, then touches of orange to the nearest one and to the pinecones. Lightly fix before attending to the final details.

6 *Finished picture:* 13½ x 9¾″

Add yellow highlights to the pumpkin, gourd, poppy pods, and pinecones. Add brighter yellow patches to the wheat. Blend the yellow background into the blank paper at the top edge and feather orange into the bottom edge.

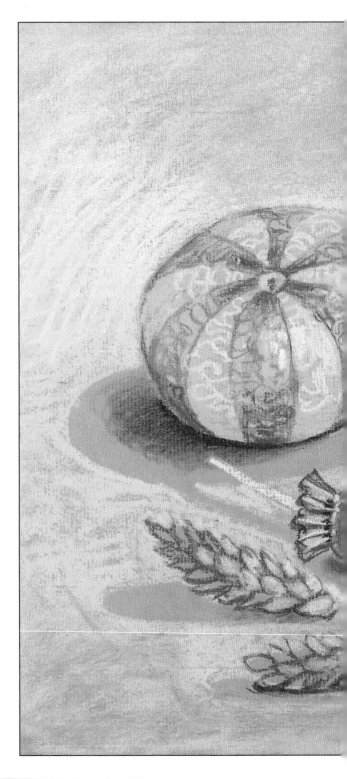

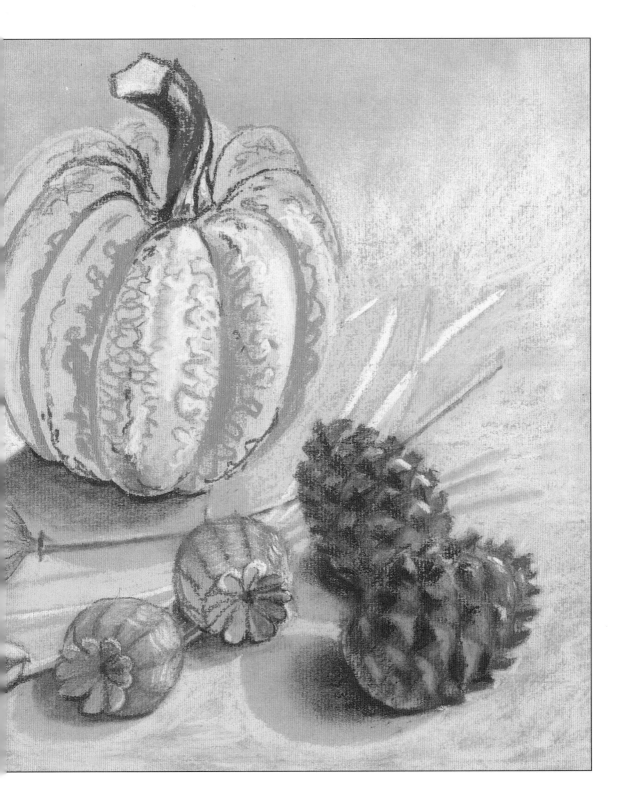

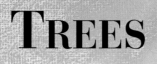

TREES

In a sketchbook, make brief studies of various species of tree through the year. Concentrate on just one aspect at a time, beginning with shape and working through scale, form, structure, character, and development, in that order.

Shape and scale

Comprehensively record basic shapes and make a note of species and location—a tree growing on an exposed, windy site will look different from one of the same species growing in a dense forest.

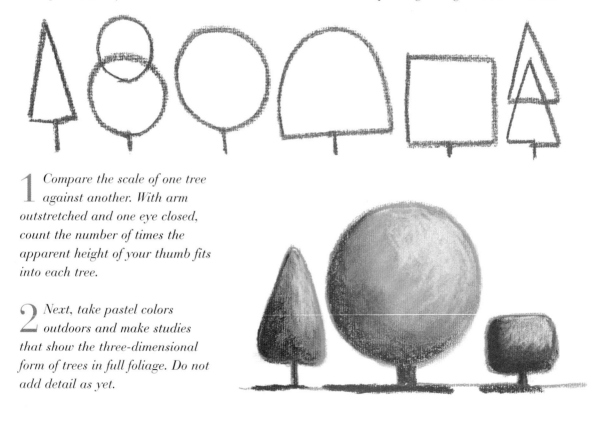

1 *Compare the scale of one tree against another. With arm outstretched and one eye closed, count the number of times the apparent height of your thumb fits into each tree.*

2 *Next, take pastel colors outdoors and make studies that show the three-dimensional form of trees in full foliage. Do not add detail as yet.*

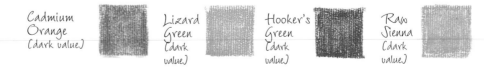

Cadmium
Orange
(dark value)

Lizard
Green
(dark
value)

Hooker's
Green
(dark
value)

Raw
Sienna
(dark
value)

Structure and character

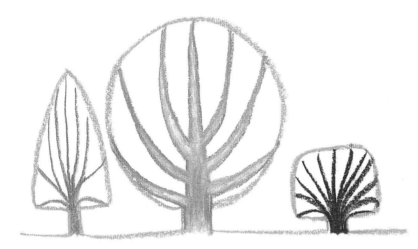

1 *Study deciduous trees in winter, when you can see their skeletons. Try to find trees with a straightforward branching system to give you an easy basis for study.*

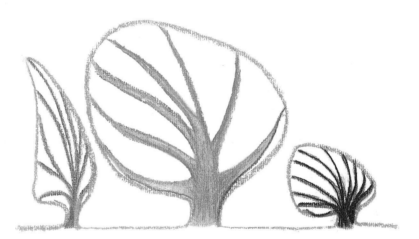

2 *Saplings adapt to accidents and weather. A perfect tree gives you the easiest start, but a weathered tree has the character that motivates a painting.*

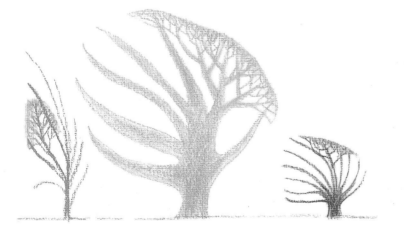

3 *Main branches have lesser branches following the same growing system. This pattern repeats itself on an ever-decreasing scale within the outer tree shape.*

Developing a tree

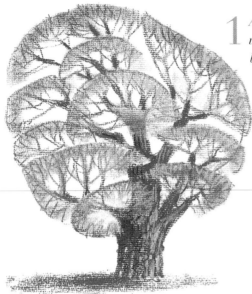

1 *Again, the time to start studying trees is in winter, when you can clearly see their branch systems. Twigs mass into clear-cut shapes; lightly drag a pastel along the outer edges.*

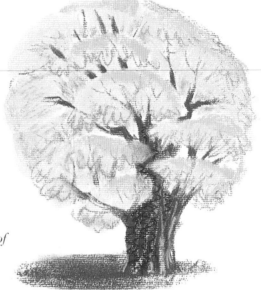

2 *Fix the first stage, then drag a thin veil of foliage color over each mass of twigs. Lightly stipple. Emphasize tonal contrasts in the branches and trunk rather than in the foliage.*

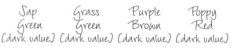

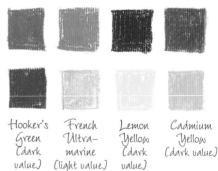

Sap Green (dark value)	Grass Green (dark value)	Purple Brown (dark value)	Poppy Red (dark value)
Hooker's Green (dark value)	French Ultra-marine (light value)	Lemon Yellow (dark value)	Cadmium Yellow (dark value)

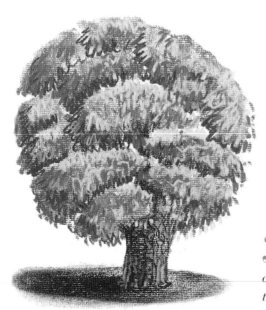

3 *Drag a shadow to one side of the tree. Fix. Stipple darker color on the underside of each foliage mass, lighter color on the side that's closest to the sun, and brighter color in the center.*

Seasonal trees

1 *Once you know how to construct a tree, seasonal changes are just a matter of selecting one of the three stages as your method and matching the appropriate colors. Winter trees are usually simple in color, the emphasis being on their tonal contrasts.*

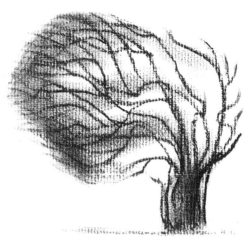

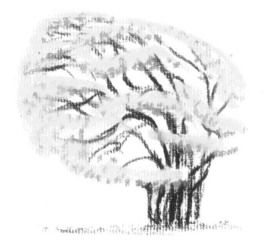

2 *The thinly clad framework in step 2 on the facing page is appropriate for spring or autumn; the difference between them is that of color. Observe the light green haze of spring foliage and the autumn colors as leaf fall begins to reveal the underlying structure of the tree.*

Terre Verte (dark value)

Yellow Green (medium value)

Lemon Yellow (dark value)

Grass Green (dark value)

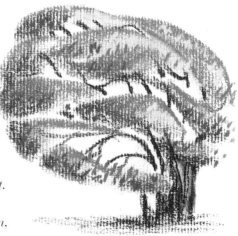

3 *A summer tree is relatively easy to draw, provided you construct its framework first. Not all species have foliage as concealing as that of the oak shown opposite; in a hawthorn, the structure is visible all year round.*

Leaves and fruit

Outdoor sketches of overall shapes are done quickly, but botanical specimens allow leisurely study at home. Such details are unnecessary for painting a tree in its entirety, but they give vital understanding of the subject.

1 *Draw outlines in colors characteristic of each set of berries, cones, buds, and flowers. Note how they compare with each other in scale.*

2 *Infill the outlines, extending the color range. The examples here show summer and autumn leaves on one twig, but ideally you should make separate seasonal studies.*

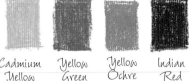

Cadmium Yellow (dark value)   Yellow Green (dark value)   Yellow Ochre (dark value)   Indian Red (dark value)

3 *Complete the study by blending and overlaying with stronger colors. Be aware of tonal contrasts of light and dark, saving highlights from the start.*

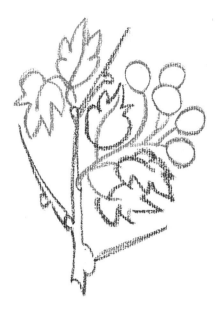

1 *Using the same method as on the facing page, draw details of a less densely foliaged tree such as a hawthorn. Small, openly spaced leaves on a twig indicate a tree that has only a light foliage canopy.*

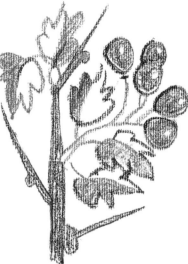

2 *Lightly infill the leaves with color, reserving half of each. Infill the berries, saving highlights.*

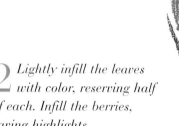

3 *Complete the infilling of the leaves, intensifying tonal contrasts. Strengthen the berries, being careful to preserve their highlights. Finally, add the long, spiny thorns.*

Purple
Brown
(dark value)

Poppy
Red
(dark value)

Yellow
Green
(dark value)

Hooker's
Green
(dark value)

Cadmium
Yellow
(dark value)

EXERCISE Paint a tree

From the studies you have made of trees, select one in a very simple landscape with level ground and a preponderance of sky such as is shown here. Using a mid-toned paper will help you to balance light and dark tones successfully from the outset.

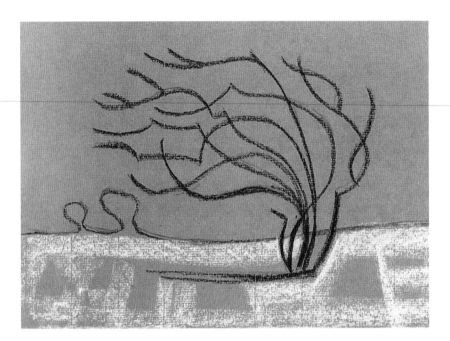

1 Draw a line for the horizon, then draw the tree from its base upwards, making sure to get its overall shape right. Drag a light color over the ground, leaving some areas of the paper blank.

2 Drag the palest color you are using over the sky—it doesn't have to be blue. Draw the shapes of the foliage masses. You can add distant trees on the horizon by simply blending them from an outline. The shadow beneath the main tree can be put in using the same method.

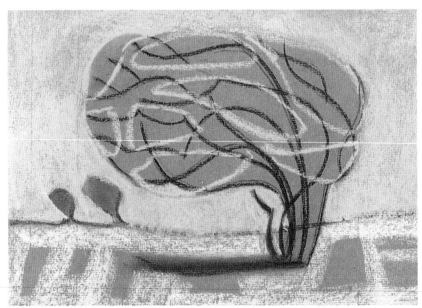

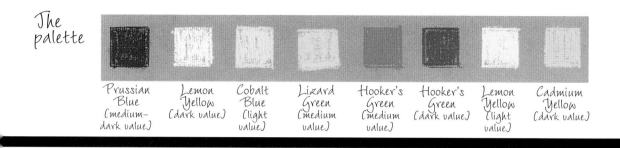

Prussian Blue (medium-dark value)	Lemon Yellow (dark value)	Cobalt Blue (light value)	Lizard Green (medium value)	Hooker's Green (medium value)	Hooker's Green (dark value)	Lemon Yellow (light value)	Cadmium Yellow (dark value)

3 *Lightly infill the foliage, leaving some blank paper. Stipple in light color at the edges of the foliage masses where the light catches them, then apply a mid-green to the center and a darker one below. Infill the spaces between them with the sky color.*

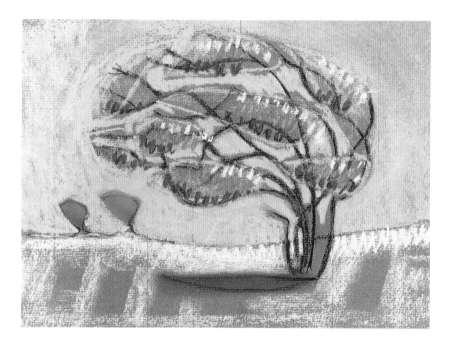

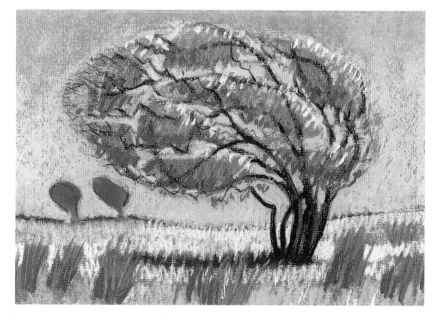

4 *Apply vertical strokes of warmer color to the mid-ground, then add still warmer color to the foreground. Stipple a similar color on the foliage to give unity. Intensify the sky color at the horizon. Finally, put in the fore-ground rushes with two tones of green.*

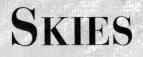

SKIES

Skies change constantly, so you are free to depict them abstractly without fear of them looking "wrong." You will already have experienced this natural and relaxed way of painting by doing the exercises on pages 16–21.

A sky sketchbook

Keeping a sky sketchbook will help you to handle pastels with confidence. Produce one study a day and note the time and date.

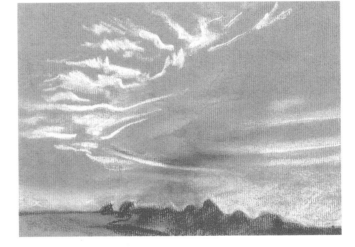

This is one of a set of studies made early each morning from my bedroom window, using white and gray pastels and a sketchbook with paper of assorted colors.

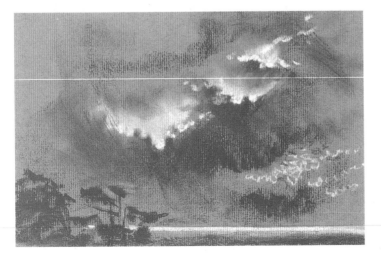

Make a study at the same hour every day for three weeks. Select a color of paper that matches the general tone of the sky, and use white for highlights and gray for darker tones.

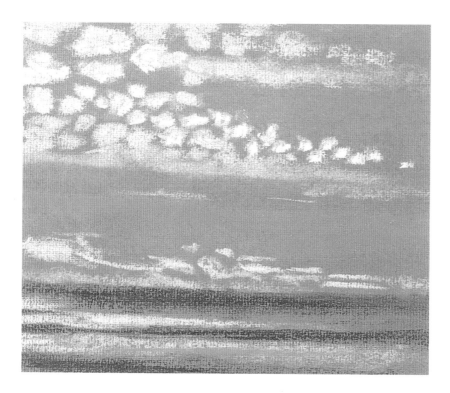

After a few days, add a colored pastel to the white and gray. Lay the broadest bands of pastel first, finishing with the smaller details. Here, pale blue was followed by gray and then white. While not an absolute rule, it is usually more effective to leave white until last.

In this sketch, gray was applied first, leaving a thin line at the horizon. It was followed by blue, yellow, and white. You will not find drama in the sky every day, but low cloud cover will give you practice in blending an even tone on the paper.

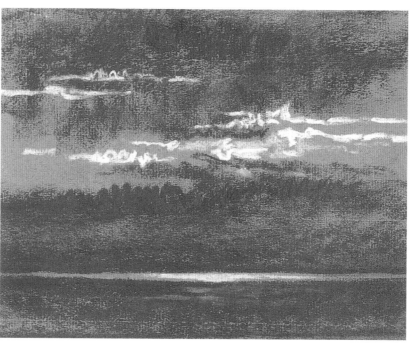

Skies on location

Try making sky studies when you are on the move— watching skies from the windows of a train offers an excellent opportunity. Here white was applied before gray. They were blended together before further accents of white were added to the tops of the clouds.

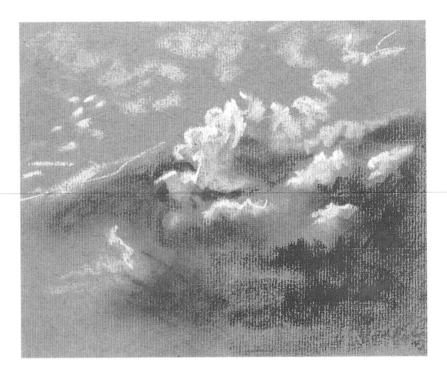

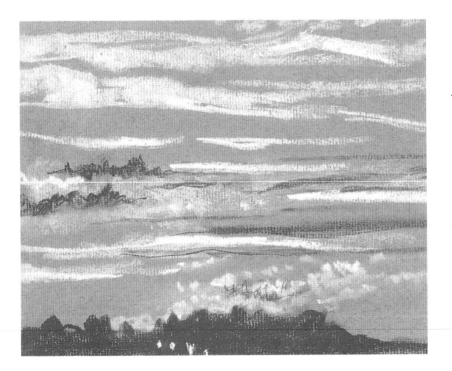

If you are tempted to record architectural or landscape features, keep them simple. It's a good idea to add some written notes so that you don't get lost in detail. Dawn and dusk are good times for sky studies, as the land is largely lost in the dim light.

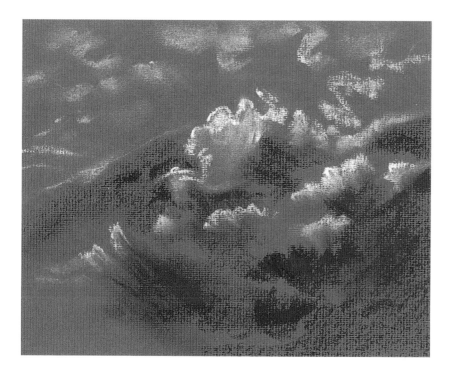

When you return home from a journey, play with your studies. Experiment with reproducing the sketches using the same pastels, but on papers of different tones and colors. You will find that you are able to change the mood of the subject.

Changing the background will also encourage you to explore different methods of creating the effects you want. Here, on dark-toned paper, streaks have been lifted with an eraser, while on mid-toned paper they were drawn directly.

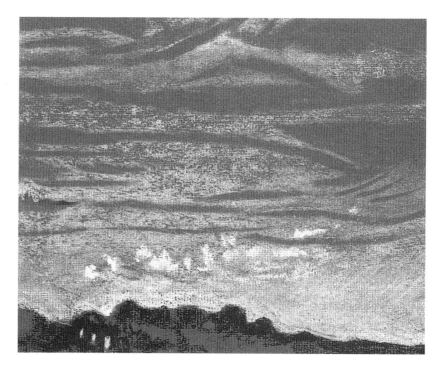

EXERCISE Paint a sky

The sky is nearest to the viewer at the top edge of the paper. It recedes in decreasing planes to its furthest distance at the horizon, where it meets the land, which has correspondingly been closest to the viewer at the bottom edge of the paper.

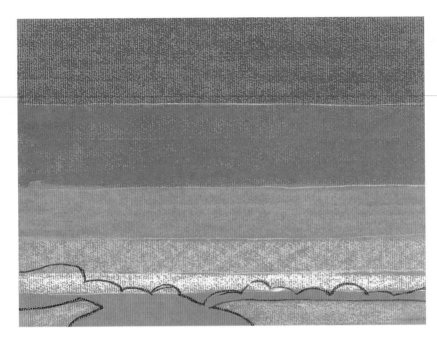

1 Divide the paper from its top edge into bands of color that grow successively lighter, cooler, and narrower as they progress towards the land. Draw trees and fields beneath it.

2 Blend the sky so that the edges of the colors merge imperceptibly into one another. Infill and blend the yellow-green of the fields and the purple-gray color of the trees.

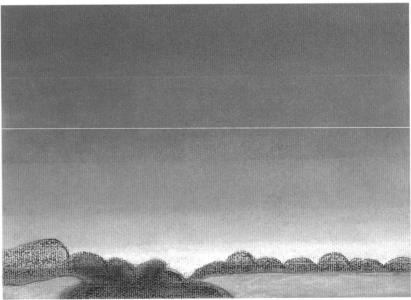

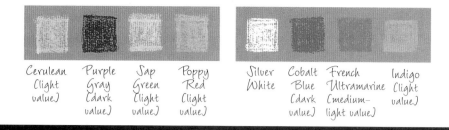

Cerulean (light value)   Purple Gray (dark value)   Sap Green (light value)   Poppy Red (light value)

Silver White   Cobalt Blue (dark value)   French Ultramarine (medium-light value)   Indigo (light value)

3 With white, lightly draw a curving grid over the sky so that it radiates from any chosen point on the horizon. Fill each space with the outline of a cloud.

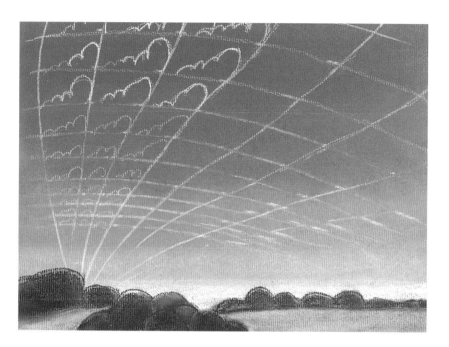

4 Blend the clouds, then feather their top edges, giving the crispest whites to those nearest the top of the paper.

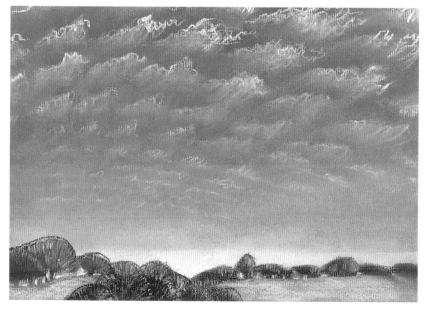

You can paint 71

AT A GLANCE...

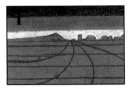 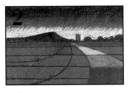 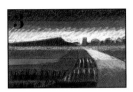 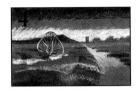

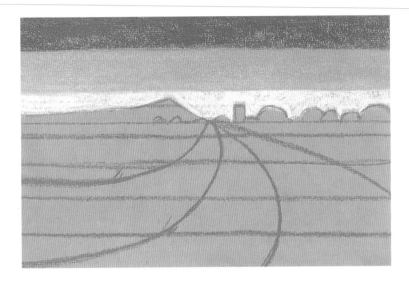

1 A typical landscape combines sky, water, trees, plants, and buildings. Taking note of the initial structures, lightly mark the position of focal points, one for distance, another in the middle ground, and a third in the foreground. Divide the sky into three bands of blue. Draw the ground planes and add radiating lines to indicate the division of path, grass shoulder, and river.

2 Drag cool blue for the hill, gray for the trees and tower, and light blue for the distant meadow. Color the path warm yellow in the foreground and graduate cooler yellows as the path stretches into the distance.

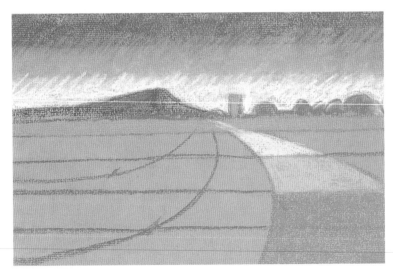

The palette

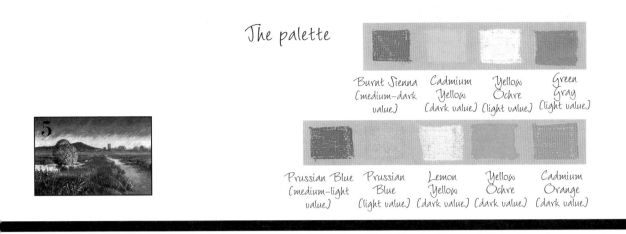

Burnt Sienna (medium-dark value)

Cadmium Yellow (dark value)

Yellow Ochre (light value)

Green Gray (light value)

Prussian Blue (medium-light value)

Prussian Blue (light value)

Lemon Yellow (dark value)

Yellow Ochre (dark value)

Cadmium Orange (dark value)

3 Loosely integrate the bands of sky, blend the yellows of the path, and drag cool yellow across the blue of the meadow. Fill areas of the middle distance with orange, reserving a space for the river. Use vertical stripes of the yellows, ochre, and blue for the foreground spaces, then blend them with a finger.

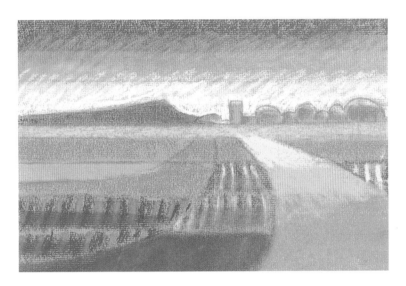

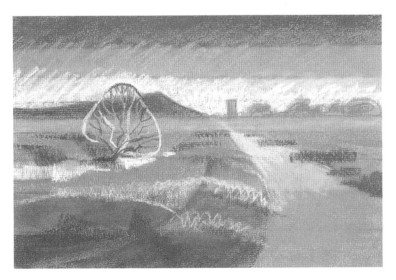

4 Draw the tree's shape and structure, using light color against the ground and dark against the sky. Block in highlights and shadows at the sides of the path. Make downward strokes of blues and cream for water.

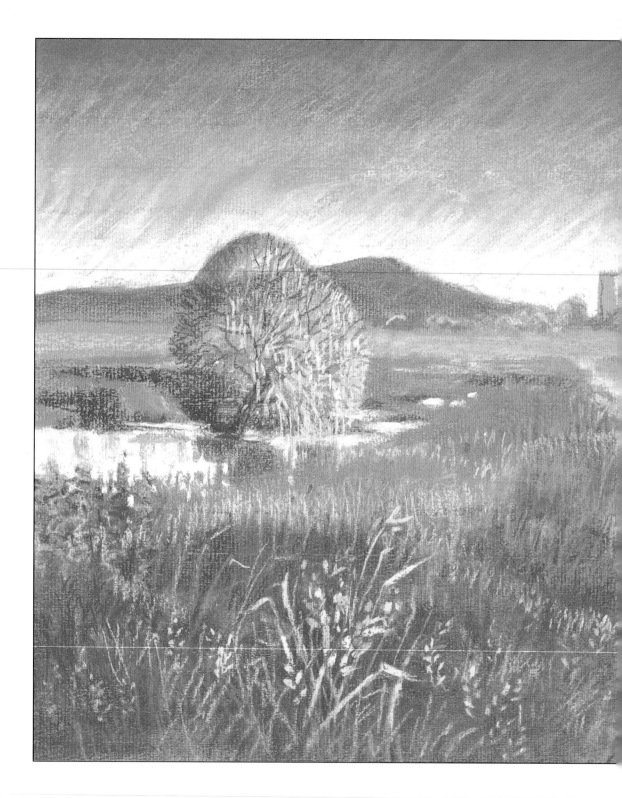

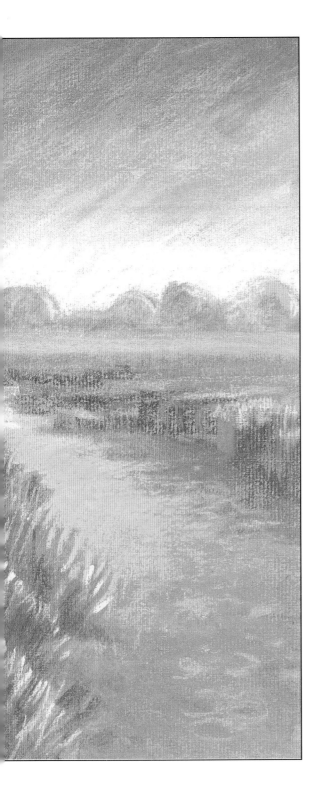

6 ***Finished picture:*** *13½ x 9¾″*
Feather the sky, path, and hill. Add high-lights to the distant view. Build the tree from its winter structure, adding a light autumn cover of vertical strokes. Add the grasses, giving emphasis to those in the foreground.

ANIMALS & PEOPLE

Earlier you practiced reflex drawing figures (see pages 20–21). For the people in the exercises on the next few pages, select a few of those drawings from your sketchbook. Animals can be depicted using exactly the same technique of capturing the moving shape without worrying about detail.

Drawing animals

Animals are no more difficult to draw than people. It is easiest to start with domestic animals and the kinds of birds you see in your backyard because their forms are so familiar. When you feel ready to explore further, make trips to parks and zoos.

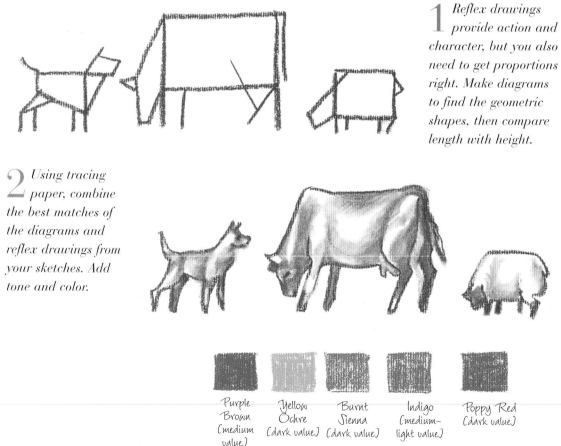

1 *Reflex drawings provide action and character, but you also need to get proportions right. Make diagrams to find the geometric shapes, then compare length with height.*

2 *Using tracing paper, combine the best matches of the diagrams and reflex drawings from your sketches. Add tone and color.*

Purple Brown (medium value)

Yellow Ochre (dark value)

Burnt Sienna (dark value)

Indigo (medium-light value)

Poppy Red (dark value)

Adding figures

Once you are comfortable with drawing and painting animals, combine them with figures. Overlap the shapes to make a convincing group.

1 *Compare the heights of animals with figures when they stand at the same distance from you. Make repeated sketches with animals of different sizes.*

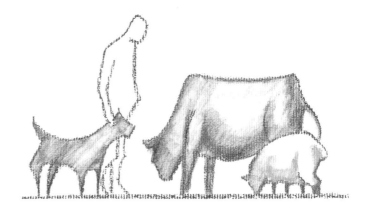

2 *The largest group is positioned on the ground plane nearest the viewer (the bottom line), while the smaller group stand on a more distant plane (the middle line).*

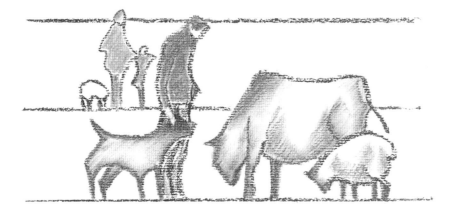

3 *The red, yellow, and blue adult figures are placed at different distances from the viewer, but they are all on the same eye level (the top line).*

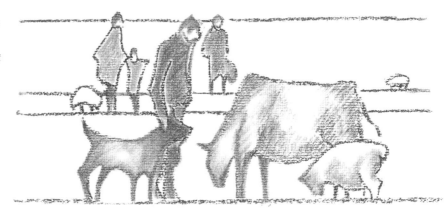

Populate a landscape

Figures, whether human or animal, give emotional meaning to a landscape. This scene is convivial, but a solitary figure can suggest more about remoteness than an empty view. Practice with standing figures and level ground before tackling more difficult subjects.

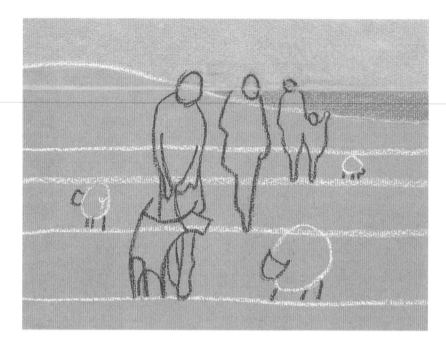

1 First draw your eye level (blue line), which will always coincide with the sea's horizon. On it, place adult heads of varying size. Draw bodies to match the head sizes and indicate the related ground planes, adding a gentle hill. Then draw the animals, keeping their sizes in proportion to the people.

2 Infill the sea, sky, and narrowing ground planes between the figures. Use receding colors from ochre to green, leaving gray paper for the distance.

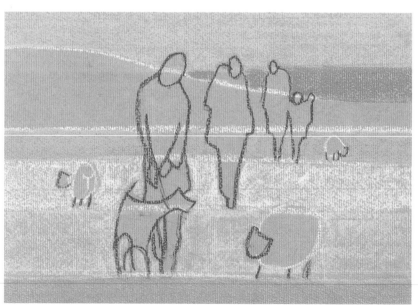

The palette

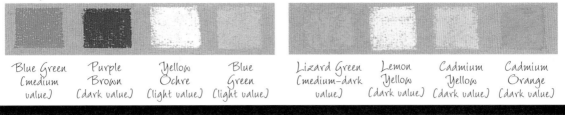

| Blue Green (medium value) | Purple Brown (dark value) | Yellow Ochre (light value) | Blue Green (light value) | Lizard Green (medium-dark value) | Lemon Yellow (dark value) | Cadmium Yellow (dark value) | Cadmium Orange (dark value) |

3 *Infill the animals, leaving gray paper for the underside of the nearest sheep. Use dark color sparingly, mainly blending it from outlines, as this gives a variegated effect and is easier to control. Blend the ground colors together.*

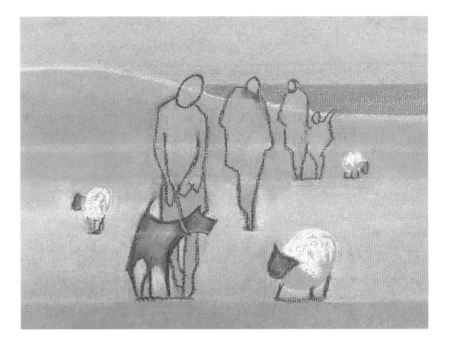

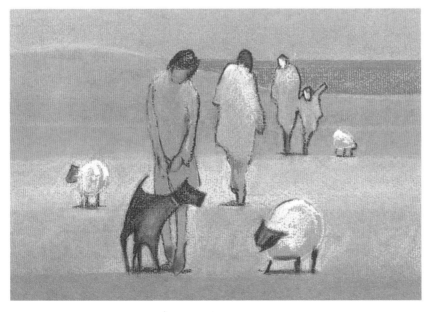

4 *Add minimal color to the people. You should aim to refine your technique of figure drawing, but in the meantime, your reflex sketches add movement to the picture. With the scene lit from above, the shadows are directly beneath the figures.*

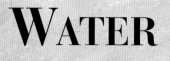

WATER

Water has no visual identity of its own—it borrows from its surroundings and from the sky. Consequently, the only effective method of painting it is by direct observation from nature and from still-life subjects. In a landscape, remember particularly to match the mood of the sky with the water beneath it.

Static water

An easy way to study static water is to draw a simple display of flowers in a clear glass vase.

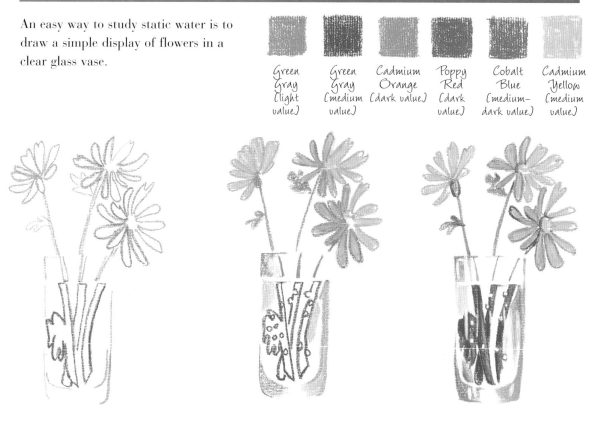

Green Gray (light value)

Green Gray (medium value)

Cadmium Orange (dark value)

Poppy Red (dark value)

Cobalt Blue (medium-dark value)

Cadmium Yellow (medium value)

1 *Draw the flowers as simple shapes. Note how the stems appear to displace behind the glass and magnify beneath the water's surface.*

2 *Air bubbles on the stalks are a further clue to the presence of water. Look also for the reflected colors of neighboring objects.*

3 *When you paint the stalks, leave vertical streaks of reflected light to indicate the surface of the glass vase.*

Reflections

Reflections vary according to subject, weather, and the stillness or movement of the water. Paint what you see rather than making assumptions about how the reflections "should" look.

1 A calm pond produces an exact mirror image. Cloud and reflection are equal in size when measured from the horizon (the top of the green band).

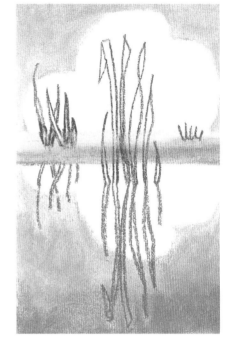

2 Rushes standing in water are reflected in their entirety. Those on the bank are only partially reflected, while those further back are not reflected at all.

Cobalt Blue (medium-light value)

Cobalt Blue (medium-dark value)

Sap Green (light value)

Sap Green (dark value)

Hooker's Green (dark value)

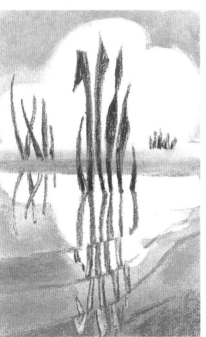

3 Water movement creates dislocated images. Notice that dark objects reflect lighter and light objects reflect darker.

Making waves

The continuous movement of the sea is initially daunting, but do not be tempted to use paintings or photographs for reference. Sit on a beach and make reflex drawings, then diagrams in color. Build your sea picture by bringing them together.

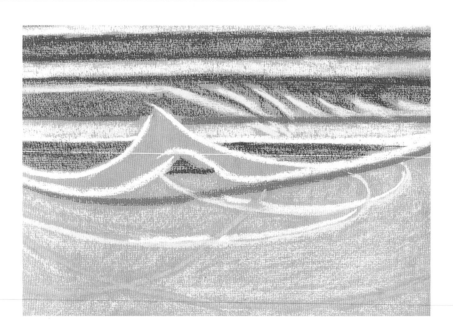

1 Make a set of diagrams from direct observation. Here, blue represents unbroken waves; yellow is rolling waves; turquoise marks the area of surf; cream is the lines of the backwash; orange marks the tidelines; and white is the surf.

2 Infill the horizontal waves with alternating blue and white, working carefully between the yellow stripes of the rolling wave. Lightly infill the sand, leaving the structure lines visible. Emphasize the cream backwash with white lines.

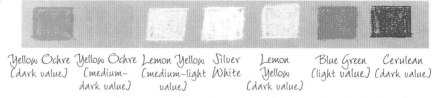

Yellow Ochre (dark value) Yellow Ochre (medium-dark value) Lemon Yellow (medium-light value) Silver White Lemon Yellow (dark value) Blue Green (light value) Cerulean (dark value)

3 Blend blue and white waves together, then interlock them with a scribbling of turquoise. Drag the curved turquoise line into the backwashed sand. Fix, then drag ochre over the wet sand, leaving gaps for reflections.

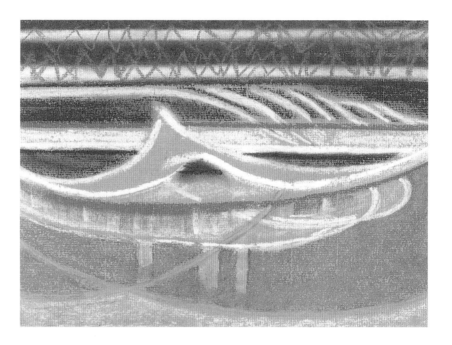

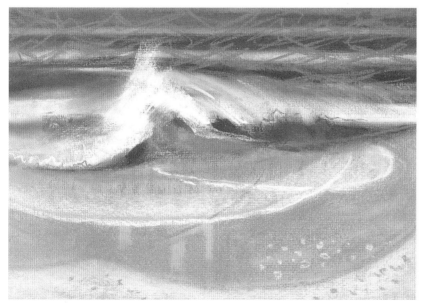

4 Blend blue, white, and yellow waves, then retouch the horizontal scribbled texture. Stipple the pebbles, using orange on cream and cream on ochre. Infill white surf from opposite directions and smudge the point of collision upwards with a finger.

DEMONSTRATION A SHORELINE

AT A GLANCE...

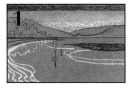 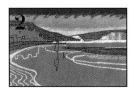 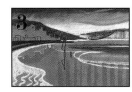 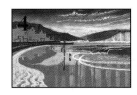

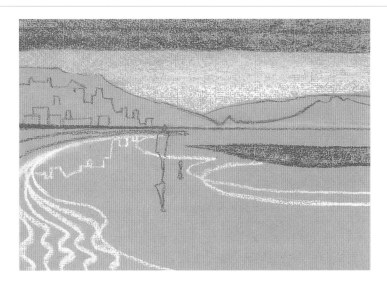

1 This low-level view avoids the complications of eye level that come with clifftop scenes. First draw the eye level, and then the figure and its reflection, the hills, buildings, curves of sand, tideline, ocean, and the town's reflection, in that order. Lightly infill the wave and the sky.

2 Infill the boardwalk and the hills with blue. Add white for the furthest edge of the ocean, the building behind it, and the valley. Pull vertical stripes of white and pale yellow over the cliff face and drag yellow across the wave.

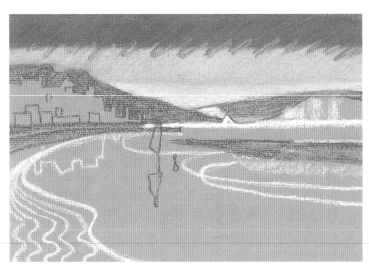

The palette

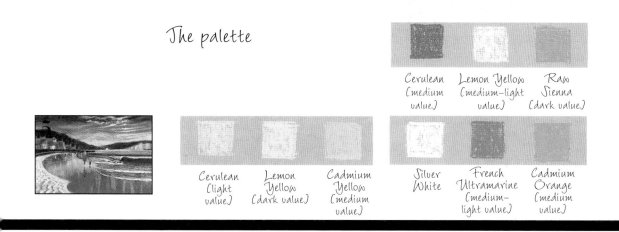

Cerulean (medium value)

Lemon Yellow (medium-light value)

Raw Sienna (dark value)

Cerulean (light value)

Lemon Yellow (dark value)

Cadmium Yellow (medium value)

Silver White

French Ultramarine (medium-light value)

Cadmium Orange (medium value)

3 Blend the sky, then lift curved stripes from it with an eraser. Infill the dry sand, leaving ridge patterns. Use ochre for vertical stripes of wet sand and to reflect the the hill above the town. Blend the wave.

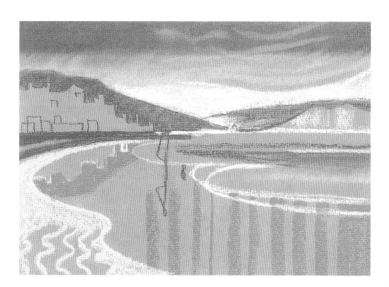

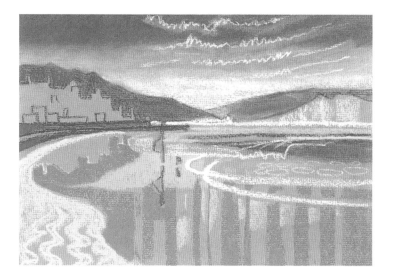

4 Highlight the clouds and surf with white. Blend the hills and add yellow, orange, and pale blue to the wet sand. Add warm blue to the left edge of the boardwalk, the hill, and the reflection of the figure.

You can paint 85

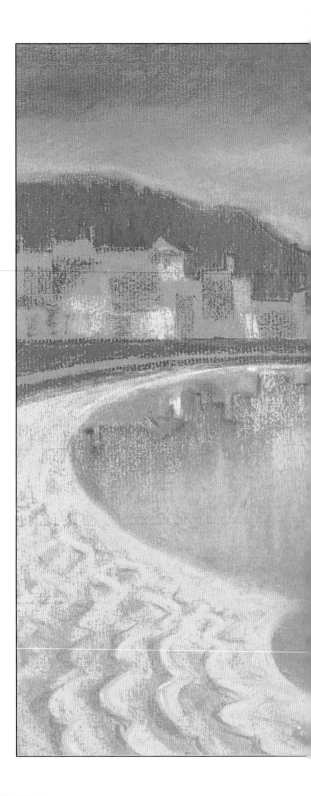

5 *Finished picture: 13½ x 9¾"*
Add minimal patches of color to the town,
dog, and figure. Drag pale yellow vertically
over the furthest area of wet sand. Shadow the
ridges of wet sand with orange. Blend the
white in the sky and ocean and put in the
reflections of the buildings.

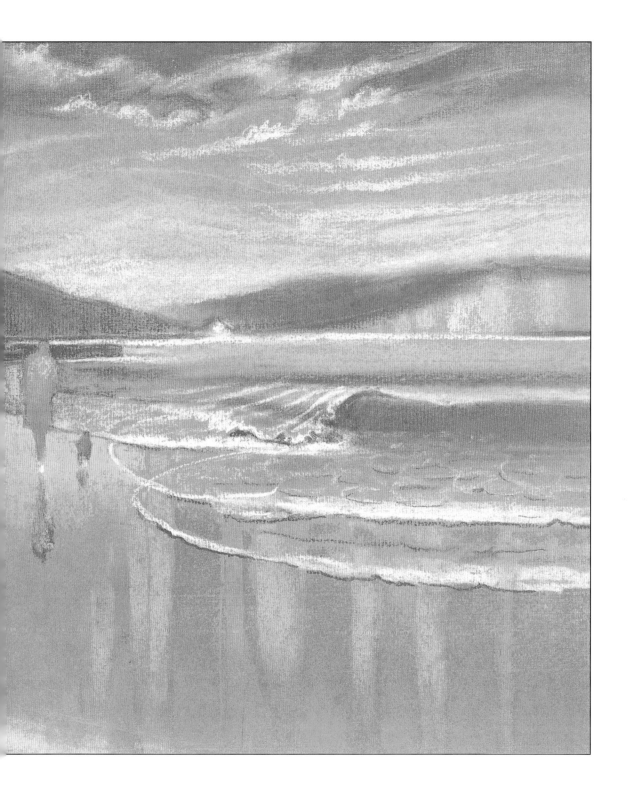

Pebbles

When we first pick up pebbles on a beach, we are attracted by their shiny, wet surface and limpid colors. These soften when they are dry, and it is then their tactile qualities that provide interest.

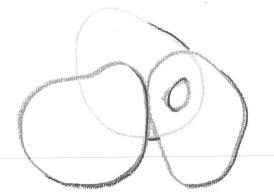

1 *Handle some pebbles and make reflex drawings. Start with blue and then switch to brown; a warm color overlapping a cool one suggests recession within a group.*

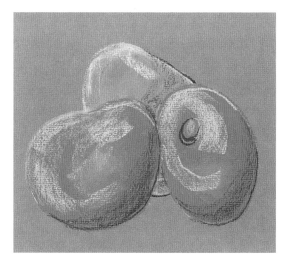

French Ultramarine (light value) Burnt Sienna (dark value) Purple Gray (medium-dark value) Purple Brown (light value)

Burnt Sienna (light value) Silver White French Ultramarine (medium value) Burnt Umber (medium value)

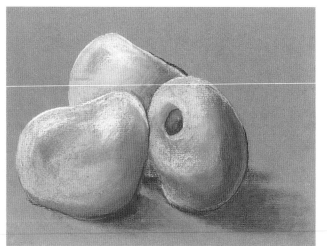

2 *Erase unwanted lines and infill color from the edges. Drag light color across upper surfaces and dark on undersides. Use blue on brown and brown on blue.*

3 *Blend colors together, adjusting the contrasts of light against dark. Add a cast shadow, but allow a gap of light to pass between the pebbles.*

1 *Take your sketchbook to a beach. Observe the way the pebbles progress from large to small and from warm to cool as they recede.*

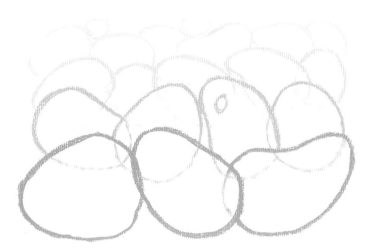

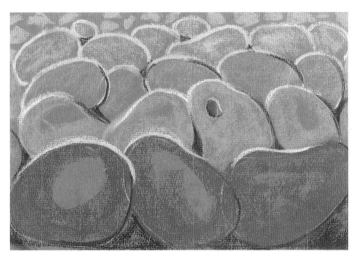

2 *Darken the spaces between the pebbles and infill the exposed parts of the pebbles, maintaining the warm to cool progression. Aim for uniformity relieved by a focus in the middle ground, which here is the hole in one pebble.*

3 *Add lighter color to the upper sides of the pebbles and strengthen the color of the shaded areas. Accentuate the hole in the focal pebble by highlighting it on one side and adding a touch of brighter color in the center.*

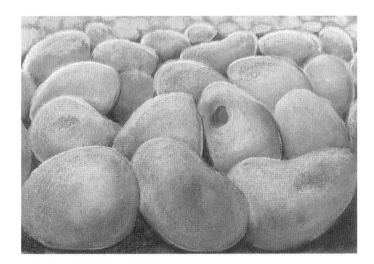

Limpets

Shells add interest to water subjects or still lifes and are attractive objects on which to practice pastel painting. Find some shells and explore their shapes and growth patterns. Limpets have contour lines like hills on a relief map, but the periwinkle is a free-flowing spiral.

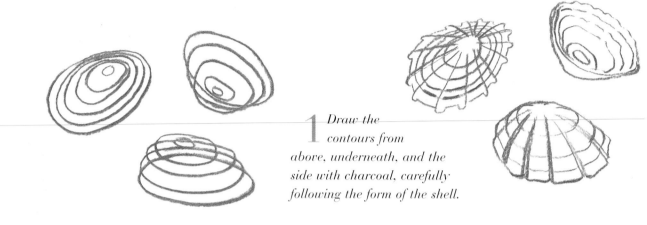

1 *Draw the contours from above, underneath, and the side with charcoal, carefully following the form of the shell.*

2 *Lightly draw visible contours and radiating lines in purple-gray. Use yellow to fill in the ridges. Add pale blue to the gray. Finally, add orange and white.*

3 *Reinforce the contour patterns by touching in with purple-gray and then adding the white highlights.*

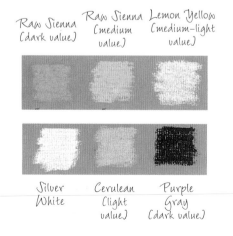

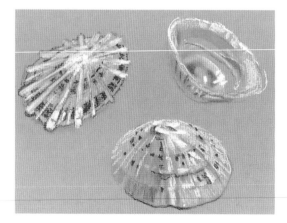

Raw Sienna (dark value)

Raw Sienna (medium value)

Lemon Yellow (medium-light value)

Silver White

Cerulean (light value)

Purple Gray (dark value)

Periwinkles

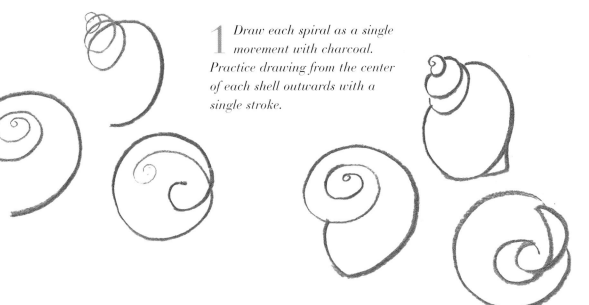

1 *Draw each spiral as a single movement with charcoal. Practice drawing from the center of each shell outwards with a single stroke.*

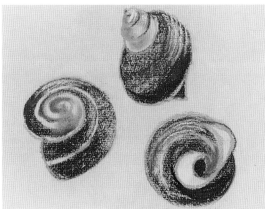

2 *Draw the outlines lightly in ochre, then use purple-gray within each spiral. Add white lines to show the surface patterns.*

3 *Blend the blue tint and touch in with the ochre tint. Complete the "ear" of the shell with purple tints and touches of orange. Add the white highlights.*

Purple Gray (dark value) Cobalt Blue (light value) Silver White

Purple (medium-light value) Purple Brown (dark value) Cadmium Orange (medium value)

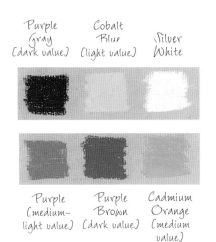

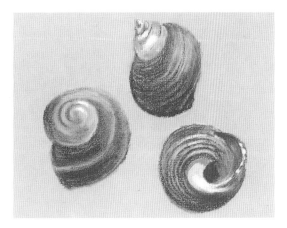

Seaweeds

There are many living organisms to be found along the seashore that are ideal for painting on a smaller scale. Free-form subjects such as seaweeds and sea anemones are satisfying to draw.

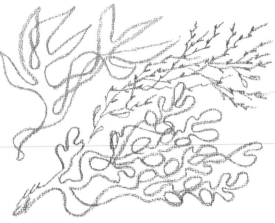

1 *Practice using a continuous line for each drawing. You will find it easiest to work from individual specimens.*

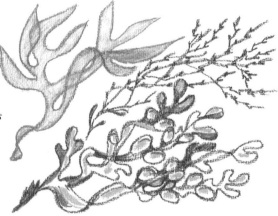

2 *Look for reds and yellows in brown seaweed. Infill the colors by blending them inwards from the drawn outlines, as shown here on the green seaweed.*

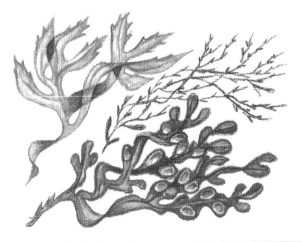

3 *Translucence is conveyed in the green seaweed by the darkening of twists and overlaps. Leave white highlights to identify the "blisters" on brown seaweed.*

Sea anemones

1 *Sit beside a tidepool with your sketchbook and draw the brown or greenish blobs that open up into the "flowers" of sea anemones.*

2 *Choose a maximum of three colors that identify each subject. Add tonal contrasts by blending and infilling outlines.*

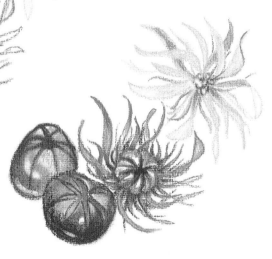

Hooker's Green (light value)	Olive Green (dark value)	Poppy Red (dark value)

Cadmium Orange (medium value)	Purple Brown (dark value)	Sap Green (dark value)

3 *Either finish at home from the sketches and notes or complete the painting on site. Lift or add highlights for shiny surfaces and add color detail.*

DEMONSTRATION TIDEPOOL

AT A GLANCE...

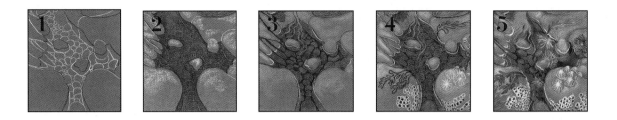

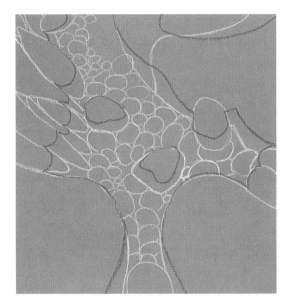

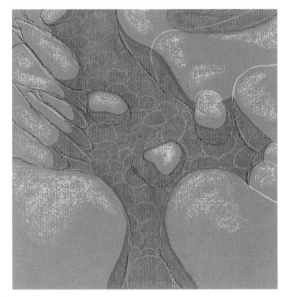

1 Tidepools combine aspects of all the seashore studies you have made. Looked at from above, they present a way of seeing that is different from our usual horizontal or vertical way of seeing things. Although recession is irrelevant, overlap pebbles from the base, establishing the direction for viewing.

2 Submerge the pebbles by lightly dragging and blending blue within the designated area of water. Drag pale yellow highlights over the projecting pebbles and rocks.

The palette

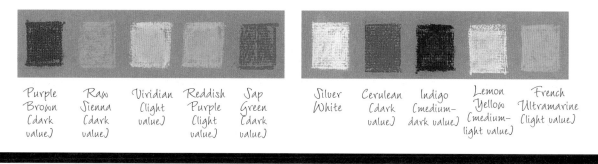

Purple Brown (dark value)

Raw Sienna (dark value)

Viridian (light value)

Reddish Purple (light value)

Sap Green (dark value)

Silver White

Cerulean (dark value)

Indigo (medium-dark value)

Lemon Yellow (medium-light value)

French Ultramarine (light value)

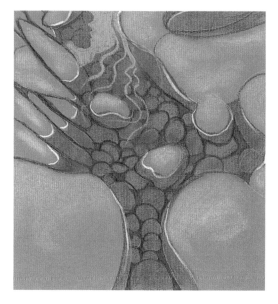

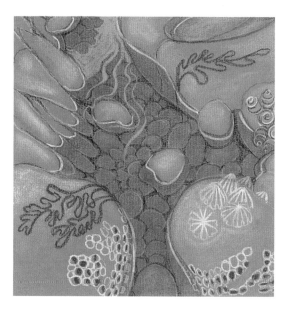

3 Blend yellow into gray. Outline the pebbles and blend into the spaces. Add a patch of ripples and reflected sky. Next, add a white outline at the water's edge.

4 Seaweed and shells add texture and give form to the rocks. From above, shells are seen full circle, but they graduate to profiles on the downward curve of the rocks.

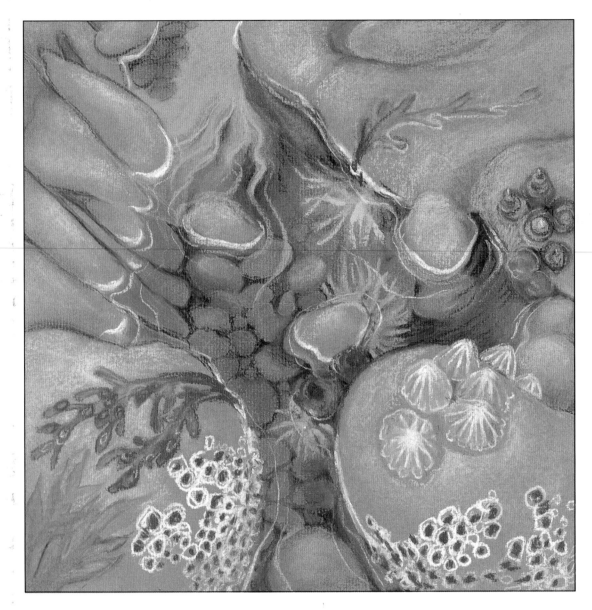

5 Finished picture: *9 x 9"*
Sea anemones in flower will be below the water. Partially blend them with blue and superimpose ripples. Closed anemones may sit
above the water level. Complete details such as the reflections and the infilling of the seaweed and shells in the way you learned from the individual studies on the previous pages.